Dragonfly's Question

Principles for 'the good life' after the crash

**A novella and discussion course on
sustainability for
communities and companies**

by Darcy Hitchcock

The Dragonfly's Question—Second Edition

Published by Lulu. ISBN 978-0-557-05409

Contents

Acknowledgements

Many thanks to the following people who provided support and advice.

Alda Barfield
Amy Brooksbank and her green team at Harry's Fresh Food
Duke Castle, The Castle Group
Michele Crim, Portland Office of Sustainable Development
Chris Dillon
Miranda Hitchcock
Libby Johnson McKee, Bainbridge Graduate Institute MBA student
Marie Morgan
Meg O'Brien, Northwest Earth Institute
Jennifer Shirley
Marsha Willard, Int'l Society of Sustainability Professionals

And most of all, my husband, Dale Graham, who didn't complain when I worked in the evenings to download this book out of my head from wherever it came.

Prologue

"As long as the people of your culture are convinced that the world belongs to them and that their divinely-appointed destiny is to conquer and rule it, then they are of course going to go on acting the way they've been acting for the past ten thousand years. They're going to go on treating the world as if it were a piece of human property and they're going to go on conquering it as if it were an adversary. You can't change these things with *laws*. You must change people's *minds*. And you can't just root out a harmful complex of ideas and leave a void behind; you have to give people something that is as meaningful as what they've lost—something that makes better sense than the old horror of Man Supreme, wiping out everything on the planet that doesn't serve his needs directly or indirectly."

—*Ishmael*, by Daniel Quinn

Chapter 1: Resurrecting Rifts

Eight years in the future....

Tess had been daydreaming while weeding her garden. She almost couldn't believe it now that she and Mark had made love in a flower-studded meadow in broad daylight on Mt. Adams the weekend before. Now she blushed, wondering what might have happened if a hiker had come upon them. But they'd been far off the trail near a whispering brook. She remembered how safe she'd felt then and later that night as they watched the Milky Way spray a sparkling path to infinity across the onyx sky. She literally trusted him with her life when they climbed rock faces but yet still kept him at arms length in her life.

She was mulling that paradox when her i-All personal communicator rang. The number looked vaguely familiar but she didn't recognize it at first. She brushed the dirt off her hands and answered the call anyway. "Hello?"

For an instant, she thought no one was on the line. "Hi, Teresa." Only her father called her that anymore.

Tess missed a beat. "Dad? Good heavens, is that you? Is everything all right?" Since she had left home, these calls always seemed to be the harbinger of bad news: cancer, prognoses, hospital visits, a funeral.

"Yes, everything's fine. I just wanted to call to say hi."

Yeah, right.

There was a long pause. "It's been a long time."

Her jaw tensed and her eyebrow arched. "Yeah, you could say that."

Her father sighed into the dead airspace. "You know, this was the one thing your mom asked of me before she …"

"Dad, she died two years ago."

"I know, I know. I just wasn't sure if you wanted to talk to me after the funeral. You know, that was quite a blow-out we had."

No kidding. How could she forget? Screaming at him at the top of her lungs in front of everyone. Of course, the argument hadn't been about the *real* issue. It never was. That was something too terrible to say out loud, an accusation so incendiary it was too dangerous get close to the fire. Better to bury the angry embers under ash and hope that someday it would die down for lack of air.

"So if nobody's dying this time, why *are* you calling?" There was an intake of breath on the other end of the line. She wanted to kick herself. She prided herself on being kind and compassionate. She just couldn't find it in herself to be that way with her father. What was it about being around your family that made you regress to teenage insolence? No matter how angry she still was with him, no one deserved that sarcasm. She wasn't a kid anymore. *Grow up. Be nice.* She forced herself to take a few cleansing breaths. "I'm sorry. That sounded harsh. I'm just wondering why you're, um," she tried to find a neutral phrase, "reaching out…now." She grimaced, wondering if it sounded as stilted to him as it did to her.

Joe seized the opportunity. "I was hoping to come see you."

Her jaw dropped. *You must be kidding,* she thought. She searched for a way to head off this train-wreck.

When Joe didn't say anything, his words tumbled like rocks down an embankment. "You see, the brokerage is merging. Again. This time, I'm the one who's redundant. They've offered me early retirement and I'm going to take it."

Tess didn't know whether to be politely consoling or shout for joy. He'd been a stockbroker — sorry, investment advisor, as he would insist she call it — as long as she could remember. His relentless pursuit of money had long been a source of conflict between them. "You? Not work?" She snorted. At least they weren't talking about a visit anymore. Maybe he'd drop the idea.

Dragonfly's Question

Joe apparently took that as an encouraging sign, an acknowledgement of their relationship. "You know me too well. You're right. I can't see myself playing golf, at least not for fun."

Tess remembered ruefully how he had forced himself to learn only to schmooze with the country club set. *Whack a stupid ball around a pesticide-soaked golf course, just to get at their trust funds.* She shook her head, dumbfounded.

"At least now I've got time to come see my little girl."

Damn! She needed to stall for time. "I'm 28 but still your little girl, huh?" *Won't we just fight?* He'd never approve of her lifestyle.

"How 'bout it?"

"Gosh, Dad. Things are a little busy. How about I drop in next time I'm on the East Coast?"

"Oh, do you have a trip coming up?"

No, I try not to take gratuitous flights that belch greenhouse gases, not like you. "Not right now. But you never know...." Maybe that would satisfy him.

"Well, good, 'cause I already got my tickets."

Shit! "Oh, wonderful," she said, trying to sound like she meant it. "When?" *How about after hell freezes over?*

"About three weeks. I didn't want to impose, though. I know this is short notice. I figured I could do some sightseeing when you're busy. Can you suggest a nearby hotel?"

Something in California would be good. Tess knew this was his way of asking if he could stay with her, or his secretary would have already gotten him a room somewhere. There was no way she could stand having him in the house. He'd complain that her house was too small, and it only had one bathroom. The thought made her shudder.

"Since you're coming in mid-June," her mind raced, "you could stay in my CCP." That way, he wouldn't have to be underfoot all the time. She could still get away.

"CCP?"

"Community Crash Pad. It's a special program here in Portland. I remodeled most of the garage, turning it into an apartment. Julie and Jennifer, the two PSU students are moving out soon since it's the end of the school year."

"You know, I could send you money if you need it. You don't have to take in roommates."

There was so much he didn't understand about her life, her values, sustainability. "It's not about money, Dad. Everything isn't about money." She sighed, reining in her annoyance. It took so little for him to set her off. *Maybe this isn't such a good idea, letting him come,* she thought. But she couldn't think of a way to stop it that wasn't down-right rude. Riga, her God-knows-what 55-pound mutt nudged her anxiously. Tess stroked his silky ears and her tension deflated a bit. His comical face made her smile. *I think I'm more likely related to you than him,* she thought.

She decided she might as well explain. If he was coming, he'd better start learning now. And acting the consultant kept the daughter at bay. "You see, Portland was having a number of problems and this CCP program solved a bunch of them at the same time. Remember how I tried to explain my work on sustainability, how it is about making decisions that have multiple benefits: socially, economically, environmentally? Well, this is like that. It's a new twist on the 'granny flat' program they tried in the '90s."

"So what is a C.C.P., exactly?" He picked at the initials like a child with a plate full of broccoli.

Don't let him bait you, Tess coached herself. "Because there has been such a demand for housing here and the population has continued to grow, Portland needed a way to provide housing but without enlarging the urban growth boundary. They also didn't want to change the character of the neighborhoods. During the last decade, they focused on redevelopment, brownfields, but that only got them so far. And they gave up on HUD ever stepping up to the plate to build more affordable housing."

She knew silence was never a sign of concession. She could just imagine his expression, bewildered and disapproving. "So they started this CCP program. Homeowners can remodel an existing building, their own house or a garage, to create a separate housing unit. The City offers low interest loans to encourage people to do this. Then you put your place and your rental criteria on the City's website. There are basically four types of people who can rent a CCP: students, low-income or disabled people and the homeless."

"Tell me you're not renting to drunks and drug addicts!" He sounded both shocked and genuinely afraid.

She rolled her eyes at Riga. "No, I decided to accept female college students only. The City conducts a full background check which helps weed out people with serious behavior problems. It also provides a healthy subsidy. So the renters benefit by having a relatively inexpensive place to live and the homeowner gets a nice source of additional income."

"Mmm." Tess knew that meant he wasn't convinced and still didn't approve. "Isn't it awkward to have someone on your property? College students, don't they have parties and raise a ruckus? What about your privacy?"

"A CCP is sort of half way between a roommate and a renter. It's understood that they should keep a low profile, help out, that sort of thing. It's actually been great having Julie and Jennifer here. When I do need to go out of town, they take care of Riga. Sometimes we take turns cooking meals. They help me in the garden."

"Well, I'm glad you liked *them*, but what if you get a loser next time?"

Is that what you think of people who can't afford your neighborhood? She caught herself. *Let it go, Tess.* "The program has relaxed a number of the tenant-landlord laws to make this work. You can evict someone for something even fairly minor—like playing music too loud—on only the second warning. The renters know that they have to toe the line because any evictions go on their record in the website."

Joe was silent, but Tess really wanted him to understand. *C'mon, Dad, get with the program. Try to see the world through our eyes.*

"This has so many benefits, Dad. Lots of elderly people have CCP's because it helps them stay in their homes. They get first dibs on nursing students—actually, any medical students—because the renter can keep an eye on them, make sure they're taking their medications, do errands. There's also a big effort to train the unemployed to be companions and caregivers so they can live and work in the same place. There's a woman down the street who gets free care in return for providing room and board. She'd never be able to afford in-home care otherwise. And rather than isolating all the low-income people into one part of town where they all have the same problem, this disperses them amongst others who might be able to help. Two other people on our street got jobs this year because of connections in the neighborhood."

"But doesn't this drive up crime? You've got all these undesirables moving into your neighborhood. At least it's gotta drive down your property values."

Ah, the undesireables again. Like there are two kinds of people in the world, your kind and riffraff. "Actually, crime has gone down. Ghettos tend to cannibalize themselves. Here, it's harder to get a gang together. There are too many eyes and ears. And when they live in a nice area, most people want to keep it up. I actually felt safer having the girls here on the property. And I think their parents were glad that there was an adult in the picture for them as well."

"Okay, so I can see how this program might help some people…."

Tess cut in before the inevitable yeah-but. "And it allowed us to have higher density, preserving open space and habitat, but without changing the look of the neighborhood. You know, up until this program, the amount of square footage per person had more than doubled. This brings the average number of people per lot closer to the numbers Portland had in the 1950's, *without* forcing people to live in the same space or cramming funny-looking in-fill housing into the neighborhood."

"But how can the City afford this? It sounds expensive." He was always on the watch for Big Government Programs.

Tess chuckled. *Got ya!* For once, she could beat him at the money game. "Actually, the university did a study and found that it was saving the City money over all. Fewer prisoners. Fewer homeless people scaring off customers so business tax revenues went up. Fewer gunshot victims showing up at the Emergency Room without insurance. Fewer elderly in nursing homes on Medicaid. Less unemployment. It was certainly cheaper than building more low-income housing and then managing the misery. Some studies show that a homeless person can cost the city $100,000 a year. For that, you could rent them an apartment, get them treatment and still have money left over to send them on a fabulous vacation! See what I mean about sustainability yielding multiple benefits? The City started this because Metro finally got tough and wouldn't extend the urban growth boundary. And instead, it solved lots of other problems too."

Tess could hear someone speaking to her father.

"Teresa, my assistant just reminded me that I'm late to a meeting. Even though I've got a bad case of short-timer attitude, I better go." He paused and his voice sounded odd when he spoke again. "It really has been great to hear your voice. I've missed you."

Tess dodged that like a toreador. Finally resigned to seeing him, she said instead, "Have your assistant send me your flights. I'll meet you at the airport."

"That's not necessary. I'll rent a car."

"Don't!" Tess said it more emphatically than she had intended, rousing their familiar power struggle. She forced herself to soften the tone. "You really won't need it."

This is going to be interesting, she thought as they both said goodbye. *Clash of Civilizations, here we come.*

Chapter 2: Culture Shock

Normally Joe would never talk to the passenger next to him on the plane. But the woman reminded him in some ways of a kindly but refined grandmother. Maybe, if he really thought about it, starting up a conversation had more to do with being nervous about seeing Teresa. Like he did with most anxieties, he just stuffed it deep into a recess in his gut, exuding confidence in its place. It was a technique that served him well during Bear Markets and especially after the Crash. Keep a positive attitude, tell people things will turn around, and hang onto the accounts.

"She's been out here in Oregon for almost eight years now," he was explaining. "I thought she'd do something more with her MBA than have a tiny consulting business out of her house. She seems to be sidelined right now doing underpaid, do-gooder work but she's boardroom material. She's really sharp."

"You must be so proud of her," the woman murmured sweetly.

But he wasn't. That was the problem. It's not so much he wasn't proud of *her* as he wasn't proud of what she did for a living and how she lived. The woman was searching his face intently, a question crinkling her brow.

"I am, but I know she can be more. Much more. And she's been dating this bureaucrat for a few years now. How's that supposed to help her get ahead?"

His aisle mate avoided the question. "Have you met him?"

"No, although I think I might on this trip. I want to size him up myself. I honestly don't know how serious it is. I just hoped she could do better." He paused. "I'm coming to visit because I want to convince her to come work with me." The woman's eyebrows twitched but she didn't say anything. "She's got a great head for business. And people warm to her quickly. She'll be a great investment advisor. People will trust her. Then she'll be able to earn what she's really worth. And," he arched a brow provocatively, "I have a host of well-to-do contacts that include some very eligible bachelors." The woman didn't say anything, just hummed a non-committal response. Joe sighed. "I figure this is my last chance to get her back on track."

The woman in 12A paused, clearly uncertain whether she should put her thoughts into words. She tilted her head up a bit to focus on his eyes through her no-line trifocals, assessing his openness. "If I had to guess, you were raised in a poor family."

Joe was shocked, both that she would say something like that to a stranger and also that she might guess. He'd spent so much of his life trying to fit into the upper class. His clothes, his car, his watch; they were all designed to hide his meager roots. Everything but his Plain-Jane new name that his parents gave him after coming to America in hopes he'd fit in. Joe. GI Joe. How ironic. He should have changed that with the rest of his personae.

The woman noticed the angry flush on his neck. "You'll have to forgive me. At my age, I say whatever I want."

Joe controlled his visceral reaction. She didn't mean harm. She couldn't know how much that hurt. His parents had escaped the Soviet occupation and came to this country when he was a child. They didn't speak English well and times were often tough. "Why would you think that?" he asked without conceding any ground. His father, who had been a respected engineer in Latvia, had to work menial jobs in the US the rest of his life. The melting pot back then was cruel to diversity, preferring vichyssoise over bouillabaisse, intent upon pureeing people until indistinguishable and uniformly White.

"Oh, usually it's the people who had to scrape and scratch for the basics who are so focused on getting rich."

Joe's stomach felt vaguely queasy but he assumed it was because the plane had just started its descent.

The woman patted his arm. "Well, money isn't everything, you know. I think most Americans still don't know the word 'enough.' And I was in the rat race as much as anyone." She touched her expensive gold necklace self-consciously. "It's like we think the economy is an end in itself. The news always reports on the Dow Jones and the NASDAQ as if they are measures of our well-being. We all forgot what we want an economy for." She ruffled her cropped white hair and sighed. "At my age, things look different. I worked so hard to earn it but it's starting to sink in that I can't take it with me."

Joe reacted defensively. How dare she lecture him about money and the stock market! This was his bread and butter; it's what made the world go around. The capital markets fueled economic expansion around the globe, lifting people out of poverty. It's what paid for Teresa's education and the nice house she was raised in. Think of all the misery the Crash of 2008 caused around the world. Was she questioning his love for his only child? This old bitty was really getting on his nerves now. "Maybe not, but it can make life here on Earth a whole lot better."

She opened her mouth as if to say something, but the pilot's voice interrupted their conversation, telling the passengers to prepare for landing. The moment allowed the tension to diffuse a bit.

She nodded inwardly as she pulled a book from the seat pocket and slipped it back into her bag. Joe noticed the dragonflies on the cover. "It's for my eight-year-old granddaughter," she explained. "She's nuts about them. She was telling me how a relative of the dragonfly—I'd never be able to pronounce the name, but she can—lived 320 million years ago, back with the dinosaurs. I thought she'd appreciate this book. I was reading in here," gesturing to the book in her carry-on, "that they spend most of their life as larvae in the water, molting repeatedly, going through a gradual metamorphosis until they finally emerge from the pond to spread their wings. So they're not like butterflies that go into a pupae stage; they change gradually over time. And they're the fastest insects. Some can fly 38 miles per hour!" She put her fingers to her lips as if to hush herself. "Oh my, I'm starting to sound like her!"

Joe chuckled, his anger largely dissipated, but a queasy unease remained. He was about to face his toughest customer yet. He thought Teresa would get over her rebellion once she got past the teenage years. He never really understood what she was so angry about all the time. If anything, he was the one who should be mad. He worked long hours to pay for the best schools so she could have the best opportunities. And now look at her. Look at what she was doing with her life. It was time to patch things up between them and get her on the right track. This was too important. It was time she grew up.

"Well, Joe, I hope your visit with your daughter goes well. I know my relationship with my kids changed so much once they became adults. Maybe that'll help smooth over your past differences. I'll hope for the best for both of you."

The escalator deposited Joe and his carry-on at baggage claim. He looked around for Teresa and finally saw her. She looked so much like Carol when they got engaged, it took his breath away. She waved and headed through the crowd toward him. Irrationally, Joe yearned for her to fling herself at him like she did when she was five, thrilled to see him at the end of a long day, her superhero who could do no wrong. It was usually after her evening bath, so she always smelled like baby shampoo and salty sea foam.

Teresa gave him a cursory, obligatory peck on the cheek. He fought the urge to clutch her fiercely to his chest. "How was the flight?" she asked now at arms length.

"Oh, fine. I consider myself lucky to get out on time in the summer with the violent storms we've been having. That's why I took such an early plane."

There was an awkward pause. "Okay, then. Let's go." She held up a small slip of paper. "I've got your Max ticket already."

He looked at her quizzically. *You must be kidding. We're taking public transportation?*

Teresa misinterpreted his hesitation. "Can I carry anything?"

Joe caught himself. *Don't criticize. Start off on the right foot. There are more important battles to wage here. And if I get what I came for, she'll be able to afford any car she wants.* He forced a smile. "Nope, got it, thanks."

Within a few minutes, the light-rail train pulled into the terminal. After just a few stops, they got off at the Hollywood station and then waited. Joe fidgeted, eyeing the other passengers warily. He was surprised to see so many professionals. In his hometown, buses were only for low-income and indigent people, and heaven knew, there were still a lot more of them around his city after the Crash. The global economy was still dragging itself out of the pit it created the end of the last decade.

Two minutes later, their bus arrived, but it wasn't like any Joe had seen before. It was three sections of bus connected by accordion pleats. "Good grief, what's that?" he asked when it pulled up.

"It's called bus rapid transit, BRT," Tess explained. "It's like light-rail but on tires. The main routes have dedicated lanes and they control the stoplights, so they are actually faster than driving. If I'd picked you up by car, we'd still be on the freeway now."

Joe noticed she was babbling on like she did when she got nervous. Maybe deep down, she still hungered for his approval. He wanted to touch her, to tell her he wasn't the enemy, but he didn't dare.

In a couple minutes, they got off at an old brick school. Joe pointed at the large array of solar panels on the roof.

"The whole community owns them," Tess explained.

What an odd idea, Joe thought. Private ownership was always the best way to go. "Why not put them on your own roofs?"

"It made more sense to put them all in one place with good solar access. We have a lot of trees in our neighborhood. We only need one inverter, and the school gets a fee for leasing their roof space. That's better for the kids than selling Coca Cola in vending machines."

Joe noticed that she couldn't resist the dig since she knew he still owned the stock. He let it pass. He had more important matters to address.

She was still chattering away. "This generates about 20 percent of the power our neighborhood uses. When we signed the contract to put them in, the power cost a little more, but thanks to gyrating natural gas prices, they're actually a little cheaper now."

They turned the corner onto her street. The neighborhood looked like a country lane with big banks of flowers and plants. The small patches of grass here and there looked like they needed a good dose of Weed 'N Feed, but most yards brimmed with verdant shrubs and trees. The tension released in Joe's neck as they walked along the yards. The houses were puny compared to his own, but the street itself was lovely. The sidewalk didn't run perfectly parallel to the street; instead it meandered along the parking strip, weaving around stately old trees. Most of the parking strip was like a marsh, filled with semi-aquatic native plants, flowers, and cattails. Two swallowtail butterflies spiraled toward the sky in an amorous dance.

A Rufous hummingbird chirped as it whizzed past Joe's head so close he could feel the breeze from its wings on his cheek. "Oh, forgot to warn you. That's the Red Barron," Teresa explained. "He thinks he owns this place. He dive-bombs anyone who comes close to his flowers."

Joe was charmed. "The street. It doesn't look like something in a city."

"You like it?" asked Teresa.

"Yeah, I think I do."

Teresa visibly relaxed as the belt of stress around her diaphragm loosened a notch, letting her take the first deep breath since picking up her father. "This was one of the early green streets. The swale captures all the rainwater off the street and it also cleans our graywater from the houses."

A young woman waved to her from the other side of the street. She had the cappuccino complexion of a complex genealogy. That and her long, wavy dark hair would have made her look exotic if she didn't look harried. Joe thought it odd that her kid was in a stroller. He looked a little old for that.

Teresa yelled, "Hey, Martha, how's Trevor feeling? Better?" The mother nodded yes and crossed her fingers, walking on.

"Graywater?" Joe asked after a short pause, trying anything to keep the conversation going, hoping to get Teresa to relax some more. *At least that should be a safe topic.*

"You know, water from the shower, washing machine and sinks, not the toilet. The water slowly percolates into the soil."

"Sort of like a neighborhood wetland?" Joe offered, thinking that would please her to use an environmental analogy.

"Exactly! We think it's a lot prettier than most wastewater treatment plants, too; don't you? And cheaper."

A little two-seater electric car rolled up and a man stuck his head out. "Hey, Tess, is the potluck this weekend?"

"Hi, Frank. Yes, it's at Ginny and Ralph's this time. You coming?" Frank was the affable middle-aged father of the Korean family down the street.

"You bet. See you then!" He rolled up his window and then turned the corner onto the main street.

Joe busied himself by looking at the intricate color palette inside one of the water irises, annoyed by all the interruptions. "Friendly neighborhood," he said, not meaning it. *God, what is this? Oklahoma?*

Teresa smiled and nodded, not picking up on his veiled sarcasm. "Yeah, it wasn't always that way. But you'll see. The monthly potluck is this Saturday. We'll go together."

Yeah, whatever floats your boat, Joe thought. He was still intrigued with the bioswale but perversely wanted to find a flaw. He couldn't believe the Health Department bureaucrats would ever go for this. He'd fought all the government fiefdoms trying to develop property and he knew they were risk-averse and mostly wanted to cover their asses. The easy answer to anything unusual was, "No, it's not in the codes" or "Hire another expert to cover my butt."

Joe pointed to the water in the swale. He didn't want to get into an argument about the role of government—a common theme in their never-ending debates—so he took another tack. "But isn't it a problem? What if someone puts something nasty down their drain?"

"Well, it's no different than with your wastewater treatment plant. Most of it eventually ends up in the river. They don't take most of the pollutants out of the water, you know." That had never occurred to Joe but he wasn't going to admit it. "Shampoo, face cream, paint, detergent, drain cleaner. It all ends up in the rivers or in the so-called compost that they then spread on farmland to be taken up by the crops. What's different here is that we get immediate feedback. The plants are our canary in the coalmine. If someone's plants start to yellow, we know there's a problem right away. And people are more careful about what they buy when they know the water is being discharged onto their own property."

Tess squatted down and turned over a rock. A salamander skittered away. "Amphibians and insects are also an early warning sign too. Wait till nighttime. You know the spring peepers we used to have when I was a kid?"

Joe nodded. "Yeah, I miss them." He and Carol used to sit on the patio after putting Teresa to bed, listening to their throbbing love-calls.

"Well, I don't know how these guys," she pointed to the salamander's tail as it slipped under a log, "and crickets got here in the middle of the city. Now we have a whole evening chorus. It makes you wonder if spontaneous generation is really possible. Instant frogs, just add water."

Joe laughed, shaking his head. Teresa always had loved science. Here she was, still playing in the mud with lizards and spouting scientific terms.

The vibrant colors, scents and textures made him feel good. Then he looked around, puzzled, because something didn't fit the image he had formed about her house. "I thought you said that you had a vegetable garden in your front yard."

"Oh, you thought I'd have a big rectangular scar on the ground?" Joe nodded and shrugged apologetically. "The garden's here; you just have to look." Teresa pointed out the raspberries and blackberries along the fence. A sign encouraged neighbors to pick them.

Teresa pulled a raspberry from its ghostly stem and handed it to him. "It's okay. I don't spray."

Joe popped it in his mouth. The complex flavor exploded against the roof of his mouth, tart and musky, like an old Cabernet. "Mmm, good!" he muttered. "I'd forgotten how great these taste."

Strawberries edged the walkway, their colorful fruit peaking out from under the leaves. Teresa pointed at a couple shrubs. "Blueberries are really a lovely plant. They're a nice size and the fall colors are spectacular." Melons and cukes flowered on a wire sculpture in the garden. "We call it edible landscaping. I would say half the plants in the front are useful for something." She pointed out the herbs—rosemary, thyme and lavender—and her semi-dwarf apple tree grafted with four different types of apples. "The rest are native plants for wildlife and flowers for the Red Barron."

It smacked of a hillbilly to Joe to put your vegetable garden in your front yard, but Teresa's was so well disguised, he figured it didn't detract from the property values. Certainly the landscaping had captured his attention so it satisfied the need for curb appeal. But his mood quickly soured as they turned up the driveway and he finally focused on her small house. There was nothing impressive about it. Just a 1940's bungalow. It looked in good shape, but still, it bugged him that his own daughter didn't live in a neighborhood more prestigious and fitting, like the one he made sure she grew up in. Appearances mattered. Didn't she know that?

He was glad his carefully chosen friends couldn't see this. They'd think he hadn't brought her up right. She could live better than this; Carol left her some money. It seemed Teresa was always trying to reject their lifestyle. Why she preferred to live in a cramped house in a lower middle-class neighborhood was beyond him. But a frontal assault would never succeed. Once he got settled in and had a handle on what her life was like, he was sure he could find a way to sell her on coming back. So he bit his tongue and bided his time.

Chapter 3: Trash Talk

The next morning, Tess left her father with his jetlag, a cup of coffee and access to her computer. She figured he could check messages and read news stories while she went to her appointment. She was grateful for the meeting because it broke up the time with her father. There was only so long they could be nice to one another. So far the visit had felt like two punch-drunk boxers circling the ring warily, neither wanting to take the next swipe, yet knowing the fight was inevitable. *Not bad for 15 hours,* she thought, glancing at her watch, even if they'd been asleep for half of them. *Only nine and a half days to go.*

She'd spent a couple hours with her client—a 'late bloomer' in Tess's lexicon—helping them compute their carbon footprint and develop a plan for becoming climate neutral. The meeting had gone well with the client committing to sign the Net Zero pledge, reducing their greenhouse gases by 50% immediately and building a plan to be climate neutral in 10 years. It was hard to believe that there were still companies out there that thought this was hard to do.

As she returned home on her bicycle, she was surprised to find her father roaming around the backyard with a sack of something, in a snit. He frowned at her appearance: her slacks tied at the ankles to protect them from the bicycle chain, some damp tendrils of hair by her ears.

He shook his head as if to say, how can this be my kid? *Here it comes,* she thought. *Go ahead, you know you want to. I dare you.*

Instead of voicing his disapproval, he held out the bag and shook it. "Where the hell is your garbage can? I've looked all over."

Tess pulled off her bike helmet and fluffed her hair with her fingers. "I don't have one." She said it with pride.

"Very funny."

"No really, we have no garbage service."

"Then how do you throw things away?"

"Dad," she said, putting her hands on her hips. "Just where do you think 'away' is? Your 'away' is just someone else's backyard. Here everything either gets recycled, composted or taken back by the manufacturer. What are you trying to throw 'away' anyway?" She could tell the little quote marks she made in the air only annoyed him further.

"Garbage. Stuff," he huffed.

"Let me see." Tess sighed and reached for the bag, peering inside. If he wasn't ready to lob the first grenade, she could keep the pin in for a little while longer. "Okay, I should have probably explained the system here before you went to bed last night. See those yellow bins? Paper goes in the paper bag. Pretty much anything else that's not compostable goes in the other one: plastic, glass, metal, etc. Some people use a green bin for food scraps; they go to the biogas plant to help generate electricity. Anything else gets taken back by the manufacturer through one channel or another."

She pulled out a Double-A battery. "There's a container for household hazardous waste near the store, a couple blocks down. They recycle all types of batteries. We'll drop this off when we pick up some things for dinner."

"This seems like a lot of work," Joe sniffed.

You would think that. It was all I could do to get you and Mom to recycle paper! "Like I always told you, it's much easier to separate things when you toss them than later, when it's all in a jumble in a landfill."

"Certainly, there must be some things that you can't just put out in your little yellow bins," he huffed.

"If it's sold anywhere in this state, it has to be taken back by the manufacturer. Actually that's true in Washington and California too. British Columbia started the whole thing with their product stewardship legislation way back in the 1990's. They required carpeting, paints, pharmaceuticals, and lots of other products be taken back. We wanted to do something similar in Oregon but had trouble with the large corporate lobbyists. Then we heard that California was thinking along the same lines. So the three states colluded, for lack of a better word, to write legislation that was basically so similar, it made the whole west coast from Baja to BC one large trading partner."

"The Left Coast," Joe sniped, his shorthand for liberals and government regulation.

"Business should be grateful. Heck, Xerox learned years ago that they could save billions of dollars by recycling or 'upcycling' parts from one generation of equipment to another. What's happening here is like a new Domino Theory. Once one product falls, others start to follow suit. What we did was stop playing the one-product-at-a-time game and just passed a blanket regulation, giving manufacturers five years advanced notice to make it happen. They all whined at first, but ironically, now they admit it's forced wonderful new innovations in product design and the smart ones saved a lot of money."

"If it's such a great idea, why don't we have this on the East Coast?"

"Probably for the same reason the whole US didn't have product stewardship legislation for about a decade after Europe— legislative inertia. The European Union had rules on the books covering everything from toasters to BMWs. Together, these three states, plus the Province, created a trading block big enough the industries had to play along."

"So that's why I can send back my old computer," Joe mulled.

"Yup," Tess confirmed. "Now it's harder for us to export our toxic trash to China."

Tess separated the waste into the appropriate receptacles and then introduced her father to the worm bin. "Food scraps go here and my little army of red worms makes fertilizer for my garden." Riga trotted over to put his head in the bin. "Back," she firmly ordered her dog. "Unfortunately, Riga thinks this stuff is just yummy so keep the bungee over the lid."

Joe wrinkled his nose. "Yuck!"

"Yeah, it's a little gross now, but here." She opened the other container and pulled out a handful of what looked like dark, rich soil. "Smell that."

Joe reluctantly lowered his nose toward the brown stuff in her hand. He shrugged. "Smells like dirt."

"Right. Fabulous soil. This is what comes out the backsides of the worms after they eat all my garbage, along with some waste paper. I mix this into my garden and the plants love it."

Teresa could tell this was all too Birkenstock for him. Edible gardens. Wastewater in the front yard. No garbage cans. He'd be on overload. He wouldn't be able to let it go.

"So what about big things? Furniture? Construction waste?"

"The entire Metro area has a zero waste goal. Manufacturers have had to figure out what to do with their 'legacy products,' the ones purchased before they could design them for disassembly and reuse or recycling. Construction used to be a major source of waste, but contractors are required to recycle or reuse at least 95 percent of their demolition waste and many exceed that. And yes, there are occasionally other things left over, usually brought in from elsewhere or from a company that is no longer in business. The City holds an occasional household clean-up day, sort of like your household hazardous waste collections. But a lot of that stuff gets used by artists. Did you notice the elk statues outside the airport? There used to be several horses made from driftwood. Eventually those disintegrated. So the same artist made the elk from old plastic lawn furniture. They'll be there forever. We're not to 100% zero waste as a community yet, but we're darn close. What's left over can usually be burned for electricity."

Joe just shook his head. Tess had to remind herself that he was used to putting out a 30-gallon trashcan every week without thinking about the consequences. He thought it went to that magic land of Away. *You don't have to live next to Fresh Kills,* a landfill so large it's visible from space, one of the largest manmade structures on earth. *What do you care?* There were so many elements to the sustainable lifestyle that had been refined over time. Joe was really getting a crash course. She almost felt sorry for him. She glanced at her watch. "Hey, are you ready for lunch? There's a great sandwich shop around the corner."

Joe got an impish grin on his face, alerting Tess to an impending teasing. "Is there tofu involved?"

"No, Dad, no tofu," she replied, refusing to take the bait. He loved to tease her about eating the stuff.

"Then I'll even buy!"

Chapter 4: Local Economy

The following afternoon, Joe was reading the Wall Street Journal on the back deck of Teresa's little backyard apartment. He still preferred reading the paper version rather than the one online, even though he knew Teresa would disapprove. He couldn't imagine how two college kids lived in this small space. Thanks to creative use of skylights, solartubes, and fiber optic lights, the place was bright and cheery. But it still made Joe feel claustrophobic. *The whole place would fit in my living room*, he thought. So he sat out back, overlooking part of the garden and yard, enjoying the sun on his face.

"Hey, Dad?" Teresa was knocking on the door.

"Yo! I'm out back," he yelled.

Teresa came out onto the balcony with a wicker basket over her arm, a towel draped inside. "Tonight is the monthly neighborhood potluck."

"Monthly? You mean annual, right?"

"No, actually it's every month. Why?"

"I've never heard of such a thing. Sure, we used to have an annual thing back home. It was usually a disaster. I can't imagine doing it monthly."

Tess shook her head. "I hope it's okay but I always make an effort to go."

"Sure, I can look out for myself." He flipped the page to continue reading.

"I didn't mean that. You can come with me."

"Why would I want to? I don't know any of these people. I'll just stay here and read."

"C'mon, Dad. It'll be fun. You can meet more of my friends and neighbors." She paused. "Anyway, I was hoping you could help me get ready for it."

This was the first time in years she'd asked for his help on anything. It was not a moment to be missed. He set down the paper and monitored his tone. "Sure, Sweety. What do you need me to do?"

"I thought I'd make Mom's famous deviled eggs. Can you run down to Emily's and get me a dozen? I'm out and she always has some. She's the house with the blue shutters on the south side." She handed him the basket.

Joe felt self-conscious carrying a wicker basket. *Tisket, a tasket,* his mind mocked. Fortunately the house was only about a block away. He went up to the door and knocked. The wind chimes pealed delicately in the warm breeze. A handsome woman of about 60 appeared at the door. She matched Joe's height, close to 5'11", with smooth, alabaster Scandinavian skin, her shoulder-length white hair pulled back with a loose peach-colored ribbon a the base of her neck.

"Hi, I'm Joe, Teresa's father. She asked me to come get some eggs."

"Teresa?" She looked confused, and then her eyes widened with recognition. "Oh, yes, *Tess.* I see the resemblance now. Hi, I'm Emily. She said you were coming into town. Come on in." Joe wondered what Teresa had told her about him. Nothing good, he was sure. But she didn't seem wary. More like amused, as if she knew an inside joke.

Joe followed her into the house, expecting Emily to open the refrigerator when they arrived in the kitchen. Instead, she proceeded right out the side door into her backyard. Joe followed, confused.

Then he saw ducks waddling through the grass. "You have livestock? Aren't there regulations against that?"

Emily shrugged. "Oh, it's been legal for decades to have three chickens in the city but I prefer ducks. They have nicer personalities and they love to eat slugs, something we can have in abundance around here. Tess usually comes and borrows them for a bit. She calls them the Pest Patrol." She picked the white one up in her arms as it murmured unintelligible comments. Joe couldn't tell if the bird liked the attention or was complaining but he was struck by the intricacy of the feathers.

"This here is Bertha, a Pekin. She's the boss."

"May I pet her?" Joe reached out with the tip of his finger to stroke the bird's back, the color of fine porcelain and just as delicate.

"The others," Emily said pointing at brown birds with white spots on their faces and cobalt wing stripes, "are harlequins, great layers but quite rare. So how many eggs did Tess want?"

"She said a dozen."

"Hmm, let me see if I've got that many." Joe followed her into the shed, a pretty little grey building with red-framed wood windows, where she pulled a couple eggs from the nest, being careful to leave one. He half expected the place to reek but it just had a damp earth odor.

She took the basket and laid them carefully in the towel. "They're huge!" Joe remarked. They were twice the size of chicken eggs and covered with a waxy coating along with what he hoped was just dirt.

Emily opened up a little refrigerator and counted out the rest into Joe's basket. He couldn't help admiring the shapely curve to her fit buttocks as she leaned over.

Oblivious to Joe's attention, Emily explained, "Usually people just come into the backyard and take what they need. So next time, you can do the same. Just write down what you take in Beaumont Bucks on the clipboard there. It's the honor system."

"Beaumont Bucks?"

Emily's eyes seemed to radiate a serene joy, blue with green flecks. "Yeah, that's our local currency. Haven't you come across that yet?"

"You print your own money? I would think the IRS or the US Treasury might have a problem with that."

"It's all legal. I think there's some rule where you can't have an exchange rate between local currencies and dollars, but otherwise, it's just a method of barter. Ithaca has had one for decades." She pulled out what looked like a credit card out of her wallet. It was a dull brown color like paper bags, with two interlocking burgundy B's on the front. "You see, the way it works is you can buy stuff around here with dollars or Beaumont Bucks. Our money can only be spent locally, though, so it helps support our local economy. The longer we can keep a transaction going within our own community, the more we benefit. Have you ever read Jane Jacobs?" Joe shook his head. "Well, she wrote this book called *The Nature of Economies*. She said that nature and economies work the same way. She compared a desert to a rainforest. In a rainforest, the nutrients are recycled again and again between organisms before finally being released from the ecosystem."

Joe jumped in, "But in a desert, the energy just comes in and gets radiated back out. So that's why it's not as diverse."

She looked surprised. "Yes! That's it. Not many people get that at first."

Joe just shrugged but inside he was delighted to have impressed her. "Teresa was always watching science shows. I guess I picked some of it up."

"So Beaumont Bucks help us have a rainforest economy rather than a desert one. It helps recirculate our resources. I used to tell my students it's like a pinball game—the longer you keep the ball in play, the more points you rack up—but none of them know what that is anymore."

They shared a chuckle about the generational knowledge gap. Then Joe picked up the main thread of conversation again. It felt so good to be having a conversation untainted with a troubled history. He could relax and just be. He didn't need to worry about stepping on a long-buried landmine. "This is really interesting," Joe scratched his jaw and leaned on the rock wall by her vegetable garden. "As a financial advisor, we talk with economists all the time, but I never thought about how the economy relates to nature."

Emily snorted. "Economists! Most of them think the economy is a perpetual motion machine."

Joe liked to see the spark in her eye. He could tell they'd hit on an issue she was passionate about. And he was fascinated that someone so grounded could also be so cerebral. "What do you mean?" he asked to keep her talking.

"They think that growth can go on forever, that there are no inputs or waste. Herman Daly, the former World Bank economist, said that traditional economics was like studying the human body just through the circulatory system. No inputs, no outputs. It looks like a closed system, but we know the human body doesn't keep going long that way. Our economy is intimately dependent upon nature. So many years we all looked at the Gross Domestic Product as if it were a measure of our well-being. Well, Katrina was great. So was Hurricane Kiernan that did an equal amount of damage to the East Coast a few years ago. Cleaning up after climate change cost a fortune. So did the Iraq war. The GDP doesn't distinguish between things we want to spend money on to improve our lives and bad things like environmental clean up and prisons. Daly said the GDP is like a calculator with only a plus sign."

Joe handed her back her Beaumont Bucks card and Emily waved it in the air as if to apologize for her lecture. "Sorry, occupational hazard." Pointing to the card, she added, "These local currencies help to build communities and balance out income differences. Individuals can sell services too, offering practically anything. A person down the block is the only one with a pickup so he often runs errands for people. Gloria has been retired a long time from teaching and she loves to baby sit. So it really encourages people to help one another. It feels more like doing favors than a normal economic transaction. Most people charge 20 Beaumont Bucks per hour, so someone who does yard work can trade time with the attorney to have a will drawn up, something he could never pay for in the regular economy. And the kids can work for Beaumont Bucks too, which teaches them responsibility. That's why I got the ducks. I needed something to offer back to the community. And it's so much fun to see the kids with the ducklings. I usually get a bunch of hatchlings each to raise each year since I have the incubator." She pointed to a Rube Goldberg home-made contraption in the corner of the shed with lights and pulleys. "Oh, are they darling when they're babies! My little ducklings are all over the city now."

Joe glanced at his watch. "Hey, are you going to the potluck? What time does it start?"

"Ohmygosh, it's already 4:30! It starts at 5:00."

"Boy, where did the time go? Teresa is going to think I got lost."

"Na, we all have that problem here. It can take 20 minutes to walk down the block because you end up talking to everyone along the way. We like it that way."

"Well, I better get these back," Joe said as he reached to take the basket back from Emily. Joe brushed her fingers for just an instant when he grasped the handle. He thought he might have even seen her blush a bit.

Maybe going to the party won't be so bad after all, Joe thought as he hurried back down the street with a new spring in his step.

Chapter 5: Breaking Bread

Riga barked and wagged his tail when he saw Joe out the front window. "Glad *you're* glad to see him," Tess told him. But for reasons she couldn't explain, she wasn't mad at her father right now. Maybe she was letting her guard down since they had had only minor incursions on one another's worldviews. She smiled inwardly as she saw her father bound up the driveway. She figured she should be upset that her father took so long. It was far too late to hard-boil the eggs. But she could imagine what happened. People always got waylaid in the neighborhood talking to others. It was part of the charm of the place. And Emily, who still taught at Bainbridge Graduate Institute's MBA in Sustainable Business program, was a fascinating woman, a talker and an even better listener. *Maybe Dad's opening up a bit.* In the past, he would have been in too much of a hurry to engage in a conversation in a situation like this. He'd always been so goal-oriented. Get eggs. Get out. And the basket was so out of character! Maybe it had been cruel to give him that. He carried it stiffly, like a suitcase, his arm out to the side so the basket wouldn't bang against his thigh.

The screen slammed behind Joe as he came in the side entrance. "Sorry. Did you think I got lost?"

"No, but I think we better come up with something other than deviled eggs to bring to the party. It starts in 20 minutes."

Joe looked at the eggs and thought for a second. "What about a frittata?"

Tess brightened. "Great idea. I'll get some stuff from the garden and you start whipping up these eggs."

Tess took the eggs out of the basket, rinsed the dirt off each one, and set them in a large bowl so they wouldn't roll off the counter. Then she went outside with the basket and scissors to find some herbs and vegetables to add to the frittata. She returned quickly with a handful each of parsley, rosemary, and thyme. She also had picked several large leaves of red-stemmed Swiss chard, a yellow zucchini, and a little red onion.

"This should do it," she said. "This zucchini was hiding out under a leaf. It's kinda big, but I think it'll be okay, don't you?"

"You got all that from your garden?"

"Yeah, I've got plants stuffed everywhere." The herbs scented the air.

Tess turned on some classical music and put a large skillet on the stove. While she waited for the olive oil to heat, she handed Joe a block of cheese to grate and then quickly chopped up the onion and chard. In no time, the kitchen was filled with rich smells and lush Baroque counterpoint. As they waited for the frittata to finish in the oven, they cracked a bottle of Oregon Pinot Noir. They clinked their glasses together, smiling at their accomplishment. She glanced at her watch. It was just 5:00. "Hey, we make a pretty good team," Tess said.

"I was thinking the same thing myself," said Joe. He looked like he was going to say more but thought better of it. Tess shot him a questioning glance, but she figured he'd tell her what he came for eventually, when he was ready. It never worked to rush him. She was just grateful to have a rare, tension-free moment. *If we string enough of these together....* She didn't finish the thought.

The potluck was in full swing when they arrived. Tess struggled to find room for the frittata on the picnic table. She had put a couple bright nasturtium blossoms and some chopped flat-leaf parsley on top for decoration. The backyard was packed with neighbors. Kids were scrambling on the jungle gym while adults stood around holding glasses of wine and bottles of beer. The Asian man Joe had seen in the electric car was telling a story that had all the adults around him in stitches. Tess nodded in his direction. "That's Frank. He's a great story-teller." Frank had inherited subdued facial expressions from his Korean heritage, but he was 100 percent American—something that bewildered his parents—with a devilish wit. The contrast between the reserved Asian stereotype and what came out of Frank's mouth made it all the funnier. Gilberto, who was born in Honduras, could identify with Frank's Coming-to-America stories and was laughing so hard, he looked close to tears. Jalal, a former Iraqi translator who lived in the CCP next door, after finally being allowed to immigrate, looked uneasy about making fun of his new homeland, but given all he'd been through, Tess was just glad to see him participating.

Tess introduced her father to Ralph and Ginny, the hosts. Ralph looked like he was born with a Budweiser in his hand: NASCAR baseball cap, scruffy neck and a bit of a beer belly. No matter what he wore, he gave it the aura of a slept-in T-shirt. Ironically, he preferred bitter microbrews to a Bud, what he called horse sweat. He was partial to New Belgium in part because they were the first to make beer with solar power. He'd started drinking that brand when he was in college in Colorado and never switched. The neighbors gave him grief for not buying some of the local brews, but Ralph was a loyal customer. Ginny, his wife of 12 years, was red-haired, round and jolly with a Boston accent. She never seemed to take anything too seriously. Tommy, their ten-year old son, was a baseball fanatic and had organized a system of neighborhood pick-up games.

Ralph addressed Tess. "You going to bring that drill back any time soon?"

"Oh, right, I forgot," Tess answered. Then she explained to Joe, "Ralph here is our Tim the Toolman. He manages the tool lending library for the neighborhood."

"Not an easy job with delinquent tool borrowers like your daughter." Ralph winked at Joe.

"Oh come on, I'm not the worst, am I?" Before Ralph opened his mouth, she added, "On second thought, don't answer that."

Ralph made a zipping motion across his lips, but then continued to address her father. "We decided that it didn't make much sense for us all to buy tools and rakes and lawnmowers. I already owned a lot of the stuff anyway. So I store all the stuff in my garage and anyone can borrow what they need for Beaumont Bucks."

Tess added, "And we use the local currency to buy more tools. Like this year, we decided we needed another lawnmower since everyone seemed to want to use it at the same time, despite the fact the lawns are getting smaller and smaller. Go figure. At least we got one of those old-fashioned kind." She moved her arms like a thresher.

Ginny rolled her eyes. "He uses any excuse to get more hand tools and equipment! It's like a drug to him. Once a year, we let him go to the hardware store the way you'd take a kid to Toys R Us at Christmas."

"Anyway," Tess cut in on the familiar marital banter, "we're lucky to have him. Ralph can fix practically anything."

Ralph beamed but modestly changed the subject. "Hey, can you believe the rain last night? It never used to rain like that in summer. I really needed it, though, since Tommy has been a little over-zealous about watering the garden and I was getting worried about my water supply. I really need to put in a drip system. Fortunately, the storm filled my RainWorm to bursting."

"Rain worm?" asked Joe. "What's that?"

Ralph pointed to the bladder snaking around his foundation. "There, under the bushes." Joe saw a camouflaged, turgid tube about two feet wide and 1.5 feet high. "You lay this tube around the house. Since it's flexible, you can work it around plants or you can wind it back and forth in your crawlspace. You connect the downspout into this filter here and then the rainwater collects in the tube."

"So it's for irrigation?" Joe asked.

"No, it's my whole water supply, for the house too."

Tess jumped in. "Mark really pushed for this type of technology. The water infrastructure was falling apart and it was going to cost a fortune to repair all the pipes. So instead, the Water Bureau helped fund these systems. We all now collect rainwater for use in our houses. I'll have to show you my thousand-gallon holding tank in the basement. Some people bury their tanks in their backyard. It kinda depends on your situation which system is best."

Ralph added, "Most of these systems store about two months worth of water. Mine is gravity fed to a pressure tank and UV purifier in the utility room. We don't have a basement, so the Rain Worm made sense for us."

"You're not connected to city water any more? What happens if you run out?"

"For most of the year, we get plenty of precipitation." Ralph held his hands out like he was feeling for rain. "We only have to be a little careful in the summer since we sometimes have no rain at all for two months. People tend to conserve water as they see their water levels go down. Worst case, there is a service where a water truck can come out and top off your tank, or in my case, my Worm. It's still less expensive to do that once a year than to pay the water and sewer bills we used to!"

Joe joked, "Speaking of sewer bills, I'm almost afraid to ask what happens to the sewage around here," as he nodded toward the bioswale.

"It comes to me," Ginny answered proudly.

"What? You've got a huge garbage can filled with sludge in your backyard?" Joe sniffed in mock suspicion.

Ginny nudged him with her elbow. "No, silly. I run the neighborhood biogas plant. We generate about 40% of the power used in the neighborhood as part of our distributed energy system. We take the sewage and other waste products, turn it into methane and then run a small turbine to generate electricity. The excess heat is used by the nearby businesses in their processes."

Frank, who had come to fill up his plate again, quipped to Joe, "So eat your fiber! We need all the poop-power we can get." Ginny wore an expression of indignation but everyone else laughed.

Tess shook her head, not so much regarding the bathroom humor but more for Frank's metabolism. She couldn't believe how much he could pack away. Of course, if she rode a bike 30 miles and then taught Tae Kwon Do to the local kids, she might be able to eat as much too.

Tess picked up the main thread of the conversation again, addressing Joe. "That's why we ended up with the green street in the first place. The infrastructure was falling apart and we decided to dig things up to tie into the biogas plant." Then she turned to Ginny. "This sure has changed the work that you and the people at the Water Bureau do."

"Oh you bet. At first we were all afraid that we'd be out of work. But now we employ at least as many people installing and inspecting these home-based water and neighborhood energy systems. More, if you count all the little companies that support this. It's actually been an economic boon."

Frank jumped in. "Hey, have you seen the system the business district is putting in?"

"The Rain Store?" Ralph asked like he already knew the answer.

Ginny explained to Joe. "They had to redo the parking area anyway, so they dug it up and they fill the hole with what are basically plastic crates. So it's almost all air. Then they wrap the whole thing in a waterproof membrane. They can store millions of gallons of rainwater off the commercial buildings. Then they pave over the top and no one knows the difference!"

Ralph cared more about the environmental benefits. "By collecting the rainwater, we not only avoid the need for expensive regional water systems like new dams and reservoirs, but we also prevent huge surges of water entering the stormwater system when we have heavy rains. Ginny used to work for the old wastewater treatment center, and every year, they had periodic releases of sewage into the rivers because the system couldn't keep up. These different collection systems divert the water from everyone's roofs. With all the rain we get here, it just made sense to capture and use the water on site. This might not work in Phoenix but they're perfect here."

"But what about the winter?" He pointed to the RainWorm. "Don't these freeze up?" Joe wanted to know.

"It has to stay below freezing for a couple days to freeze it solid. That doesn't happen very often around here, especially not any more," Ralph answered. "And most people have a small holding tank or pressure tank that, if they're careful, can last up to a week."

Tess noticed that Joe had stopped listening. Instead, he'd caught Emily's eye as she came into the backyard with a plateful of her famous brownies. Emily nodded and headed toward them. "Hey, long time no see," she said to Joe.

Tess studied his reaction with horror. He puffed up in her presence like a chickadee fluffing its feathers to look more imposing. They started up a conversation. *Oh my God, he's attracted to her.* This was the first time Tess had considered that her father might be interested in a woman other than her mother. The thought stunned her. Despite all the marital arguments and manipulation, Tess always took for granted that her parents would somehow stick it out. Of course, now with Carol gone, it was reasonable to assume that Joe might date again. *But gad, can't he do it in the privacy of his own home, not in front of me?* Suddenly all the food on the table seemed unappealing. *And geeze, especially not with my neighbors!* She had to get away from him, needed time to think. She was afraid what she might say. She was disgusted by his behavior and furious with Emily to be encouraging it. *You were my friend!* In a daze, she filled a wine glass to the brim and headed toward the mass of neighbors. The crowd flowed around her, enveloping her like an embrace.

Chapter 6: Connected Communities

The next morning, Joe took his coffee in Teresa's sunroom, which looked out onto her backyard. He was still thinking about the party. *That Emily sure is something,* he thought. *Smart, good looking, fit, long legs, funny. I wonder if Teresa needs more eggs...*

Teresa walked in, grimaced at the clock and tossed her father a backpack. "It's Saturday so the Farmers Market is open. It's about a mile from here. We can walk or bike. Which would you prefer?"

Joe thought her tone was a little abrupt but let it pass. She seemed angry about something, but he hadn't been around her much first thing in the morning for a very long time. *Maybe she just needs her coffee.* "I haven't been on a bike since I was 10 so I think we better walk." Joe slipped the straps over his shoulders.

"Sure, no problem." Teresa then pointed at his slippers and snorted. "You want to change shoes first?"

Riga and Teresa took off at such a fast clip that Joe had to rush to keep up. "Is there a fire somewhere?" he joked.

"It's just Riga's dog-trot speed." But she was really walking faster than normal.

"You need a smaller dog," Joe joked.

"Good exercise. Need me to slow down?" It sounded like a challenge.

"Never!" Joe responded theatrically, smiling in mock competitiveness. However, he had to admit he'd let himself get out of shape. He'd never let Teresa see him struggling, though. Since she was six inches shorter, he couldn't get over how fast her legs could carry her. After a bit, his muscles warmed up and it wasn't so hard, but he was secretly grateful each time Riga stopped to sniff or lift a leg on a tree.

Still, conversation was sparse. There was no reason he could think of to explain her bad mood. He'd gone to the potluck like she'd asked. Hadn't they had fun cooking together? He'd been so careful to avoid explosive topics. What could he possibly have done to upset her? He wondered if she was getting her period. Carol used to get grumpy then too. He had hoped that he might be able to pop the question today, after the fun they had in the kitchen last night, but now was clearly not the moment to bring it up. Time was running out and they'd need time to plan.

Teresa led him through the Alameda area. *This is more like it,* Joe thought. The houses were large and stately, more like what he was used to. But there was one big difference. Joe was struck by how many people were out and about. In contrast, his street back home was empty of people. Perfectly manicured lawns draped front yards, but they were like his formal living room; no one ever used them. And so no one ever talked to their neighbors. You drove into your garage, shut the door, and disappeared inside.

Here, people sat on front porches drinking coffee, having breakfast, and reading the paper. Homeowners who didn't have front porches had built patios and seating areas in their front lawns. Some houses simply set out two park benches facing each other. It reminded Joe a little of the French Quarter in New Orleans where people sat out on the balconies, looking down upon the tourists. But here they were on street level so they could interact with the passers-by. It was as if a tornado had picked up all the patrons and tables from a Paris café and scattered them in the neighborhood. A little farther on, some kids stood behind tables, hawking strawberries and lettuce from their gardens. It felt so safe, so festive.

The other difference was the lack of traffic. Hardly any cars whizzed by. Instead, kids barreled down the mostly empty streets on skateboards and skates. Parents pulled red wagons loaded toddlers and groceries. The fastest thing that passed them was a gaggle of bike racers in their colorful skin-tight outfits. A Vespa puttered past with a young woman aboard, her blond hair billowing out from under her helmet.

Joe spotted a For Sale sign. "Ever think of buying in this neighborhood?" he asked Teresa.

"Good grief, no. What would I do with," she stopped to pull out a flier, "4800 square feet?"

"But your place is so small." He'd meant to make it sound like she'd be more comfortable in a larger house but Teresa was obviously sensitive to the veiled criticism.

"I prefer to think of it as cozy," she replied with a huff. "Dad, I've got 1000 square feet plus the half basement. That's plenty for Riga and me."

Her naiveté aggravated him. When was she going to learn? "Maybe, but if you want to play with the big boys, you have to live like them. It's a matter of image. You're living in a working class neighborhood," *like the one I grew up in.* "Your address affects who you know and what people think of you, regardless of what your idealism may want to be true."

"Well, I can agree with the part about where you live saying something about you. Dad, I know that having a big place probably still impresses people in your circles." Her hostility was starting to boil over. "But especially with the work I do, people would think I was a hypocrite. Around here, having way more than you need is considered gauche. No, it's more than that. People here recognize that the earth has limited resources and the world, now at 7.5 billion people and still growing, can't support us all having mansions. If everyone lived like the *average* American, we'd need five or six more earths! And it's really unclear where we'd get them. We can't all live like you. The earth can't take it."

He wanted to refute her figures. She was always spouting off some doomsday statistic yet somehow the world kept going on. People found substitutions for scarce resources. Joe remembered the dire warnings of the nutcases at the Club of Rome predicting collapse. There were always doomsayers. Why couldn't Teresa just enjoy herself? Why did she have to make herself and others feel guilty for all that they had? Joe bit his tongue because he didn't want to rile her more.

Teresa apparently interpreted his silence as staunch disagreement instead of a white flag. "And setting aside the issues of social justice and carrying capacity of the earth, just look at the price." She held out the flier.

Joe just whistled. It was an eye-popper.

"Yeah, that's one of the problems of living here. Unlike your city that is still losing people, there is so much demand, so many people who want to live here that it's driving prices sky-high. It was bad enough early in the century, but now with gas gyrating between $9-11 a gallon, all the suburbanites are desperate to move back in town where public transportation is practical. Their real estate values have crashed but ours keep going up. At least we benefit from the RFS." Joe looked at her quizzically. "The renewable fuels standard. Back in 2007, Portland passed an ordinance forcing the gas stations to mix in biofuels—which are now cheaper than gas. That guaranteed a stable and increasing demand that helped to encourage production. So we pay less to fuel up than most places."

She pointed at the sale price again. "So imagine how much harder I'd have to work to pay for this place. And I'd have to heat it, furnish it, clean it, maintain it." She ticked these off on her fingers. "It's just not worth it. I don't want to be a slave to my possessions."

Joe was searching for an olive branch. He thought of fogging, the communication technique he'd been taught in sales training years ago where you agree with as much as you can. "I guess I can see now why your crash pad concept is so popular."

If the technique was supposed to curtail the diatribe, it didn't work. "And with that extra income, I've been paying my mortgage off faster than I have to. In ten years, I should own my home out-right." She held her index finger and thumb about an inch apart and held her hand close to his face. "I'm this close to having no debt. When I'm 40, if I wanted to, I could be semi-retired for the rest of my life and still make ends meet. You always used to talk about how much money can buy. But this is real freedom."

You have no debt because I paid for your college, he wanted to fire back. But there was no point in squirting lighter fluid on the flames.

Riga tugged at his leash so Teresa put the real estate flier back in the box and they started walking again. Joe figured the best thing he could do was to shut up and let Teresa cool off. In the silence, he reflected on all the long hours he put in at the office and how much Carol and Teresa had resented his absence. It was so unfair. It was his job, wasn't it, to provide for his family? Carol had filled the emptiness with shopping. And the more she shopped, the harder he had to work to pay for it all. But hard work got you ahead, and money bought freedom in the form of shelter, food, and in Teresa's situation, a good education. Now she was taking it for granted.

Teresa sighed. "Sorry. I just want you to understand. I have what I want. I'm doing what I want. My life is meaningful because through my work, I'm helping to change the world for the better. I have time for my friends and neighbors, and time for myself. Isn't that ultimately what you want for me?"

"Of course I want you to be happy, honey. I just worry sometimes. I'm not sure you understand how the real world works."

"You and your 'real world.' Your 'real world' sucks. It's gotten us into this mess."

Was she really blaming him for the state of the world? The little ingrate. He's busted his ass to make sure that she and Carol had a comfortable life, so she didn't have to scrape and scratch like his family had. She had no idea what it was like. It was about time she grew up. She'd had it too easy and didn't know what it took to make it that way. "You can't spend your whole life trying to *find* yourself," he sneered, "taking it easy. Only the ambitious get ahead." *Was she ever going to outgrow this idealism that kept holding her back?* he wondered. "Maybe things are different here in Ecotopia," he said sarcastically, "but the rest of the world is tough and demanding."

Teresa's face blotted with angry pink patches. "Then maybe the rest of the world needs to be more like us."

Joe could feel his pulse throbbing in his temple. "And maybe the real world doesn't bend to your wishful thinking."

As the barbs came faster and more pointed, they reached the crowded farmers market. In addition to all the colorful booths brimming with produce, there were kids getting their faces painted, and a mime mimicking people. He pantomimed the two of them with a deep frown and stiff, angry movements, and Riga with his ears pulled back looking anxious. He was so sensitive and hated it if she ever raised her voice to anyone. Teresa knelt down and hugged him. "It's okay, buddy. It's not about you."

No, it's about me, the evil dad, thought Joe. No one could hurt him the way she could. And yet he still adored her. At times like this, he wasn't sure why.

Joe glanced around and was mortified to realize that others at the farmers market were watching the mime interacting with them, waiting to see what they'd do next. He desperately wanted to get off stage, to compose himself. "I'm going to get a cup of coffee. Want one?"

"Fine," she answered through thin lips.

A few minutes later, they sat down at one of the tables to listen to the music. Riga curled up under the table to protect his tail from all the shoes stomping around him. Joe tried to make a joke. "You can't just buy a cup of coffee anymore, can you? It's like it's own language." It was the closest thing to a truce he could think to say. Teresa forced a weak smile.

The band featured a petite female vocalist with a surprisingly rich, full voice. They sat in silence for awhile, the haunting melody soothed their nerves. Teresa's eyes seemed to be avoiding him.

Joe took a breath to start a fresh conversation, but Teresa sighed at the same time. "Dad, you know those big houses up there?" She pointed her nose up the hill toward Alameda as she cradled her coffee in both hands. "With the aging population, many have been converted into shared housing by seniors. So many in that age bracket are widowed or divorced that many now pool their funds with friends and buy up these places. We call them Boomer Roomers. Each person gets their own room or suite and they share the house. It's a form of co-housing. It works well because usually at least one person can still drive, another may like to do yard work, someone can open jars, and so forth."

Joe nodded knowingly. "I'm not sure how I'd feel about living with other people but I guess I can see the attraction." He was quiet for a minute. "The house is really quiet with Carol gone." He'd murmured it so quietly he wasn't sure he'd said it out loud.

Teresa gaped at him like she was seeing him for the first time. She studied him long enough to make him uncomfortable. Then she reached across the table to grasp his hand. "I'm sorry. I suppose it's been hard on you too." She looked directly into his eyes. "Tell me how you are, really. You haven't talked about it at all. I really want to know."

Joe was not used to thinking about his deepest feelings, much less talking about them, but he stepped into the doorway she held open for him, in part he rationalized, because it might soften her up for the proposition that framed the reason for his trip. He talked about how hollow the house felt without anyone. How, before he got 'outplaced,' he'd thought about getting a dog but worked so many hours, that that didn't seem fair to the dog. How, now that he'd lost his job, his main social network had evaporated; many of his coworkers seemed reluctant to talk to him as if getting laid off was contagious. Non-competition agreements prevented him from contacting former clients for business, some of whom he had known for years. And Carol had always arranged the parties and the evenings out with friends. So in the past few weeks he had spent a lot of time alone.

Teresa was silent for a moment, taking it all in. "Boy, I had no idea. Now I feel bad. I should have been there more for you. I was so wrapped up in my own grief and my own life, I never thought that much about what it was like for you."

Joe was about to say she didn't have to apologize, but Teresa was momentarily distracted by the buzzing from her i-All. "Call?" asked Joe, slightly annoyed.

"No, it's just my Smart Home system. It's letting me know that it's shutting off some appliances."

"Boy, that could mess up the Thanksgiving turkey." Joe felt relief that the spotlight was turned away from his aching heart.

"Yeah, I suppose so. But you can override it. You'd just pay more to buy energy off the grid than from the neighborhood system."

"Kinda like your own little Enron," Joe teased, knowing that would get her goat.

Teresa just scrunched up her nose as if she'd just smelled something dreadful. "As the percentage of renewable energy has risen, it's been a little tougher to match energy production with demand."

Joe nodded. "You mean like, during the Superbowl, everyone reheats their nachos in the microwave at the same time."

"Yeah, right. So rather than build and maintain a bunch of traditional power plants for peak demand like this, it's better to let the utility turn off some of the plugs. It doesn't hurt my frig or washing machine to let it sit a bit. You can program each appliance for the maximum shutoff time. And you see those plug-in hybrids?" She pointed to the cars parked on the street. "When they're plugged in, the utility can 'buy' power from their batteries if they need it."

Joe was stunned. The problem with renewable power was always the storage. The sun only shone on certain times of the day. The wind didn't always blow. Everyone agonized about the batteries you'd need to store the power until you needed it. But if you could think outside the box, there were thousands of batteries in cars just sitting in garages for hours doing nothing. It was an elegant solution! "So I guess, if the power company draws down your battery, you just drive on gasoline instead until it charges back up."

"Bingo."

Afterward, when Teresa got pulled away to talk to friends and then to shop, Joe reflected on what it felt like to share his emotions with Teresa. It was like his chest cavity had opened and dark, unacknowledged thoughts buried in his heart were able to fly away. *Maybe this is what the woman on the plane meant about having an adult child,* he thought. It was nice not to have to protect Teresa anymore and to be able to level with her.

Of course, there were things he hadn't shared. He didn't tell Teresa that she was now his main lifeline—as frayed and tenuous as it was—because that would scare her. The twin stilts that had held him above the crowd for so long—his job and his family—had both been kicked out from under him. He always knew he loved his wife, but Joe had been surprised how dreadfully he missed Carol. Sure, some of the widows were practically flinging themselves on his doorstep as if it had been smeared with catnip. But that wasn't friendship. That was raw need. *You can't quench your thirst at an empty well,* he thought. And that's just what Joe felt like, an empty well.

Except, somehow, he felt a little rejuvenated here. It wasn't his attraction to Emily; he wasn't at all sure how he felt about that. Maybe it was just being around Teresa, having family near by. But it wasn't as if they'd been having a great time together. *What was it?* he wondered. Camaraderie? No, that wasn't quite it. One word popped into his brain: Community. A sense of community. In only a couple days, he felt welcomed and accepted by Teresa's neighborhood in a way that would have been unthinkable in his own. Now all he had to do was to get his own daughter to feel the same way.

Chapter 7: Anti-Toxin

Tess was taking a short meditation break on the back patio, trying not to wonder where her father had been going when he left the CCP. She was *not* going to speculate about him and Emily. Nope. *Ooops, focus on your breath,* she reminded herself when she noticed her mind wandering again.

"That's one crappy grocery store you have," Joe said before he realized her eyes were closed.

I will not get defensive, she told herself. She let out a breath for eight counts and opened her eyes. "Mmm? Why is that, Dad?"

"Well, first of all, they didn't have any bananas. I always have one on my cereal. And, I couldn't find any of the brands of bathroom cleaner I usually use, or shampoo. I ended up getting this." He held out a bottle of Alba as if it were a dirty diaper.

"Ah, I see," Tess answered, the glow of her meditation hanging in there for the time being. "You're not likely to find bananas in the store because they don't grow locally."

"Don't tell me your City outlawed those too?"

"They're not outlawed. It's just most patrons now understand the social and environmental impacts of shipping food all over the world, and when we stopped buying so did the stores."

"You've got to be kidding. You don't ever eat bananas?" Joe was astounded.

"Actually, once or twice a year, the store will bring in a shipment as a special promotion. I tell you, when you eat seasonally, things taste so much better! It's a real treat. But no, we don't have them every day of every year like you may have in your stores."

"Well, why the hell not? Why should I have to give up my banana in the morning? It's part of my ritual."

"Okay, you really want to know?" Joe nodded but unenthusiastically. "I'll take that to be a yes. Actually there are a number of reasons. First, before we started emphasizing local produce, the average plate of food in the US traveled about 1500 miles, farther than most go on their vacations. Think of all the fossil fuels. Think of how long that took. Think of all the nutrition and flavor leaching out of the food as it drove up and down the highways. There's a reason store-bought tomatoes taste like wet Kleenex and imported mangos like turpentine."

She was counting on her fingers again. "Second, industrial agriculture has dramatically reduced the genetic diversity in our food. We've lost so many different varieties. And diversity is nature's insurance policy. Someday, we may be very sorry.

"Third are the social impacts of creating Banana Republics dependent upon a world economy controlled by day-traders. Their livelihood is tied to commodity traders in New York City high-rises and elsewhere. Better that they should be able to grow a diverse group of foods that they like to eat themselves."

"So you're still against free trade?" Joe asked in a deprecating tone.

"Not at all. Trade is fine. But it should be the icing on the cake, not the raison d'etre. Think about the problems of food security in a global world. As oil prices continue to rise and when bad things happen in the world—be it wars or earthquakes or hurricanes—it's safer if you can provide the basic necessities locally. Your community probably has a four-day supply of food. How safe does that make you feel? In my view, communities should be able to provide most of their food, water and housing materials from their own region."

Joe put his hand on his hip. "But what about coffee? You have coffee shops on every block. You and all your friends are addicted to it."

"True, true. We have to keep a couple vices. Did you know that coffee is the second most traded commodity?"

"Really? What's the first?"

"Oil, of course. Still." She shook her head, mystified. "But back to the coffee issue, at least around here it's all now certified SmartGrind."

Joe nodded, glad finally to hear a sustainability term he was familiar with. "I remember once you told me to buy certified coffee and I couldn't figure out whether you meant shade-grown, organic, bird-friendly or fair trade!"

She snorted. "It was a confusing mess, certification run amok. Anyway, regarding the local issue, despite what some caffeine addicts may think, coffee is not a necessity. It would be ugly for a week until the caffeine withdrawal subsided, but we could manage without. We can't manage without food. And that's why we've worked so hard to protect the farmland around the city and the urban community gardens in the city. After 9-11 and with the recognition of peak oil, this became an integral part of our disaster planning."

Joe harrumphed but had no come-back. "So what about my shampoo. It's made in Connecticut. I looked. Is that too far for Ecotopians?"

He was making fun of her again but she wasn't going to take the bait. "Well, you do get points off for that, but it's likely to be a different matter. Why don't you bring me your old bottle. I'll meet you in my office. I want to show you something."

Tess turned on her computer and logged on to the SEER Household Products Database at the National Institutes of Health as she waited for Joe to return from the apartment.

As Joe reentered her house, someone knocked at the front door. Tess yelled, "Can you get it?"

Shortly thereafter, Joe came in her office. "There's a Black guy at the door. Says his name is Terence."

Funny that's the thing you notice about him, his skin color. Portland had made a lot of progress but it was still harder for people of color. Tess liked having Terence and his live-in girlfriend in the neighborhood not only because they added diversity, but also because both were registered nurses. Terence had a heart of gold and had helped Tommy set up the neighborhood baseball games. He was average height but well-muscled with a magnificent, glossy shaved head. *To Dad, he must look like Mr. T without the Mohawk,* Tess thought.

"Hey, Terence, what's up?" Tess could tell immediately that something was wrong.

"It's Trevor again. Martha just rushed him back to the hospital."

"Oh no! I saw her just the other day and she said that he was doing okay. What can I do?"

"I told Martha I'd line up all the neighbors like last time. Can you take care of their dog again? The key's in the usual place."

"Of course, no problem. Anything else?"

"Not right now but thanks, I'll let you know if there is. Ginny's doing grocery shopping and cooking meals for them. I'll take care of their yard. Gloria said she'd clean house and feed the fish. So I think we're set."

"That's great. Thanks for getting this all organized. What about building a schedule for hanging out with Martha in the hospital? She's going to need some support."

"Emily's working on that as we speak. She'll post a sign-up sheet on the neighborhood website. Anyway, I've got to run, but thanks for helping again."

"Don't mention it. I'll go by the hospital this afternoon. It's too hot to bike to my client so I was planning to take the bus anyway. It goes right past there. I just hope that Trevor is going to be okay."

"Yeah, me too. He's a real trooper."

After Terence left, Joe cocked his head to ask the obvious question.

Tess sighed. "It's so sad. Martha has had a terrible time with him. He has a lot of chemical sensitivities and now he's been battling leukemia. We've helped her go through the whole house to eliminate sources of toxics. But he probably already got a pretty good exposure when he was in the womb."

"Toxics? Like what? What did she do? Drink drain cleaner?"

"Actually, you'd be surprised how many common household products still have nasty chemicals in them. You, me, all of us have hundreds of chemicals in our bodies that don't belong there: industrial solvents, pesticides, wood preservatives, fire retardants, refrigerants. Mark and his friends at the State are still trying to outlaw vinyl here but the stuff is everywhere and the industry lobby is really strong. I'm not sure if this is true but I heard somewhere that a vinyl shower curtain loses half its weight in three years after you take it out of the package. You know that vinyl smell? Those are synthetic chemicals, mostly plasticizers, that off-gas. That's what you're breathing in when you smell it. A lot of these household chemicals are endocrine disruptors, chemicals that mimic hormones. At least we banned them from lining steel cans used for food. But still, the body burden, the number and amount of synthetic chemicals Americans have in their bodies—in their blood, their tissues—is still rising. And it's not just a matter of living in an industrial society. We have about eight times higher levels of fire retardants in our bodies than Europeans."

Joe looked shocked. "How is that possible?"

"Well, Europe passed legislation, oh gosh, it must have been around 2006 or so, banning lots of persistent chemicals, especially those that accumulate as they move up the food web."

"Accumulate? What do you mean? How?"

"Well, imagine you poured a small bottle of pesticide into a lake so that the concentrations were very small. Let's say the concentrations are below the level the EPA would consider unsafe. Now all the microscopic organisms, as they filter the water or eat algae, get one dose in every mouthful. But their bodies don't recognize this synthetic chemical, can't burn it for energy or excrete it. So over time it builds up. Now a tiny fish eats many of the tiny organisms in its lifetime. And a larger fish eats lots of the little fish. And then a larger fish yet. Finally the eagle or you, at the top of the food chain, catch the large fish for dinner. You're probably getting a million times the dose of that pesticide than the concentration in the water."

"Wow."

"Yeah, wow. You remember the warnings about eating tuna, before there was the worldwide fishing ban?"

"Mercury, right?"

"Right. Mercury is naturally occurring, not synthetic, but it's not good for cells. And tuna and other large fish get a disproportionate dose because of this process, what's called biomagnification."

"So it's natural."

"Not exactly. Know what the biggest emitter of mercury is?"

"No idea. It used to be in thermometers but that stopped a long time ago."

"Coal-fired power plants."

"Power plants? I remember that China was building the equivalent of one or two coal-fired power plants a week during the 2005-2010 period. It was actually a great Wall Street play. I helped my clients buy companies that made equipment for those plants and we all made a fortune."

Joe had hit one of her hot-buttons. "Yeah, well, those plants belch out mercury and it comes in pulses across the Pacific Ocean, seeding the fisheries and even making it to our shores. So this is an example of you and your clients making money off of trashing the world."

Joe got defensive. "All of it was legal. If it's so bad, why is it legal? We can't be the watchdogs for the regulators! It's not our role."

Tess still had enough serenity from her meditation session to resist the urge to take his anger personally. It was only natural to be angry. Everyone felt that way when they started to understand.

She turned to her computer to redirect the focus. "So, tell me what brand of bathroom cleaner you were looking for." It was a common one so they found it in the database list and Tess clicked on it. "Okay, it says here, 'Excessive exposure can lead to liver, kidney and blood effects.' Hey but at least birth defects are 'unlikely.' That's a comfort," she added sarcastically.

Joe looked a little sheepish. "Okay, what about that one. I use that sometimes." He pointed to another product in the list.

"Well, it says it has a compound which, in its pure form, has been reported to cause liver, kidney, spleen, thymus and blood effects in lab animals."

Joe was feeling defensive. "Yeah, but it also says that's not relevant in normal use. So it's not a risk to me."

Tess turned toward him. "But think about it. First, the EPA tests each of these things individually. They don't test for the delightful chemical cocktail we're all exposed to simultaneously. And second, in most neighborhoods, this stuff goes down the drain and ends up in the river. So lots of other organisms are swimming in this stuff and being forced to drink it. They test these products on lab animals but every organism has its own tolerance. It's ironic that it's not considered ethical to do controlled experiments on humans but instead we're conducting an uncontrolled experiment on the whole planet. Sure, the concentrations are low, but imagine all the households in the city using stuff like this. Factories all over the world are cranking out millions of bottles a day. It adds up, especially if the ingredients don't biodegrade rapidly. Why take the risk if you can find something safer that still does the job? I just use baking soda and vinegar for cleaning most things. Sometimes hydrogen peroxide. That's why you didn't find any 'cleaning products' under the sink. You don't need any of these things." She gestured at the list of products on the computer screen.

"Okay, I can see how cleaning products could be nasty because they're supposed to kill germs, but what about my shampoo? Why isn't that in the store?"

Tess clicked on the hair care button and then on his favorite product. "Hmm, it's got glycerin which can target the kidney and liver and propylene glycol which affects the central nervous system. Oh, and wait, it gets better. It's got something that affects reproduction too."

Joe was stunned. "How can this be legal?"

"Exactly. Good question. We used to think 'the solution to pollution is dilution.' But we're finding that even in tiny concentrations, everyday products can have nasty effects. Sometimes, small concentrations are even worse because your body doesn't know to defend itself." Tess glanced at her watch. "Oh! Look at the time. We better go check on Rufus and take him on his walk." She knew his routine from past dog-sitting assignments.

On the way to Martha's house, she returned to Joe's original unspoken question. "So poor Trevor has all this stuff in his body and it's rebelling. It's making him sick. He's had a terrible time with asthma all his life and now he has leukemia. Maybe he's genetically geared to react. But all this pollution is affecting everyone. The hormone mimicking chemicals from lots of sources appear to be making kids develop faster, and the earlier girls have their first period, the more likely they are to get breast cancer later. And it's not just people. Way back around 2000, we were finding male fish in the rivers with eggs growing on their testes."

Joe instinctively moved his hands to protect his genitals.

"In 2006, studies started to show that even legal levels of air pollution were contributing not only to the epidemic of asthma but also heart disease. But Martha, and through the placenta, Trevor too, got a particularly heavy dose since she used to live in the country, near a large farm. We like to think of the country as pristine, but before converting to organic methods, agriculture was addicted to chemicals. Martha already lost her husband to non-Hodgkin lymphoma, which is directly linked to agricultural chemicals. That's why they moved here in the first place, to be closer to Oregon Health Science University. Terence acted as her patient advocate through that ordeal so they got to be quite close."

"My head is reeling," Joe said. "But I tell you what. I wish I had had a neighbors like this when Carol was sick. I didn't have anything near the support you have here."

That's no excuse for leaving her alone that day, Tess wanted to yell. It made her crazy to think about her mom, sick and alone, probably scared, drifting away with no one by her bedside. "I came *several* times to help with Mom." *Every time you had some other business trip you just had to go on.*

"I know you did, honey, and I appreciated it. But you needed to get back to your work and your life, as you should have. But I wish I'd had such a nice group of people who lived next door. This is really great."

And then there was the one time Tess balked. Let *him* take care of her, she'd thought to herself at the time. Do your duty. In sickness and in health. Get your priorities straight. He'd said that she looked better, that she was winning the fight. He'd said he never would have gone, had he known. He'd said he could probably find someone else if Teresa couldn't make it. But he hadn't. And her father always put his job first. Always. Sure, the home healthcare service checked on her that afternoon, but by then it was too late. She could never forgive him for that. The thoughts slashed like razor blades. As much as she wanted to hurl them at him, it felt too dangerous to do so.

She wrestled her anger into a smaller ball in her stomach. "You know, Dad, we all want to feel secure. In your life, you've invested in the stock market to amass a fortune to protect you. But you can never have enough money to protect you from every eventuality." *It didn't save Mom.* "Here, we invest in building a community of people who know and care about us. That way, when and if we need something, we know there will be people to help and support us. That's what a community is."

"Those two things are not mutually exclusive."

"There are only 24 hours in everyone's day. People like you who work 60-hour weeks don't have any time or energy left to invest in their neighborhoods or friends." She looked at him meaningfully but that was as close as she could come to airing her resentment. She needed to change the subject. "And speaking of which, remind me when we get home to check the sign-up sheet for going to see Martha and Trevor in the hospital. I want to go check on her this afternoon." At least there was someone's hand she could hold, someone she could comfort.

As Tess entered the garage to get the key, they could hear Rufus, a Golden Retriever mix, woof. When Tess opened the side door, Rufus rushed past them into the yard and raised his leg on a bush for a long time. "Hey, sorry buddy. We should have come sooner. Want to go on a walk? You can come play with Riga today." She glanced at her watch, calculating the time until her next appointment. "We'll go to the dog park, okay?" Rufus wagged his tail enthusiastically and woofed when he heard one of his favorite words.

Chapter 8: Harvest Barnstorm

Joe heard someone drive up to the garage so he looked over the paper where he was reading the Monday news. There was Teresa parking a sporty, nail-polish red two-seater. She honked so he came down stairs.

"You stealing sports cars now to supplement your income?" Joe joked.

"Yeah, right. Actually, this is one of the Zipcars; the Date Car, they call it."

"I can sure see why," Joe said as he admired its lines.

"The advantage of car sharing is I can rent whatever vehicle I need— a pickup, van, whatever—and I only pay for the hours I use it. I thought you might like to ride in style. This here," she patted the carbon-fiber fender, "is a plug-in hybrid E-85. You can get over 500 miles per gallon of gasoline in this baby since it's only 15 percent gasoline and 85 percent ethanol...made from algae."

"I bet that gives the Saudi family night-sweats." It was adorable. It looked a little like an old MG or the Mazda Miata. "Where are we going?"

"Put on some grubby clothes and I'll grab some gloves. I'll explain on our way out of town."

It was a lovely morning as they headed south. Even Teresa seemed in a better mood today, and for that, Joe was grateful. The undercurrent of anger kept threatening to draw them both under.

Joe was surprised how quickly city turned to farmland. Teresa explained how the Urban Growth Boundary helped to keep sprawl in check. She pointed out Mt. Hood in the

Cascade Range to their left and the Coastal Range to their right.

"So where are we going?" Joe asked again.

"They're called Harvest Barnstorms."

"Barnstorms, like the Amish building a barn together?"

"Yeah, sort of. But instead of building a barn, practically everyone now volunteers at least one day each year to help farmers harvest produce. We started to realize that agriculture dependent on cheap, migrant labor was a problem. Not only the illegal immigration problem and labor shortage brought on by the guest worker quotas, but also for the workers themselves: lousy working conditions and back-breaking work."

She paused while she exited the freeway. "So this one farmer, when he had trouble getting laborers thanks to the 9-11 immigration restrictions, decided to take 'agri-tainment' one step further. There were already farms that offered hayrides and pick-your-own-pumpkin Halloween parties and corn 'maizes.'" She made quote marks in the air with one hand. "Maizes. Get it?"

When Joe nodded, she continued. "So this farmer sold the idea to different businesses to schedule a harvest party as a kind of team building effort. His wife was a consultant so I think she may have given him the idea. The idea spread. Lots of companies and schools started to sign up. Some non-profits bring out inner city kids who might not otherwise know where food comes from. Now, since you can take home a little of the product as payment, there's a two-year waiting list at some places like the wineries."

"But not so the Brussels sprouts and zucchini farms?" Joe quipped.

Teresa chuckled. "'Fraid not. But as more people worked in the fields, we started to understand that some of this work is inhumane. It's fun to pick apples for a day but miserable for a living."

Teresa was silent for a minute while she passed a car on windy country road past fields of strawberry plants.

Joe was thinking about his back and tight hamstrings that were still aching from all the walking they'd been doing. "We're not picking strawberries, are we? I'm not sure my back could handle it today."

"No, but they're an interesting story. Before I get into that, remind me when we get home to teach you a few yoga stretches."

"Uh, I'm quite sure I can't do that pretzel position."

"You mean lotus position? I wasn't planning to ask you to; I can't do it either. I was going to suggest downward dog."

The fresh air wafting through the sunroof put Joe in a frisky mood. "That sounds like something you'd find in the Kama Sutra."

"Dad!" Teresa looked at her father with a stunned and bemused expression that tickled him. She was shaking her head as she looked back at the road. "Anyway..., to pick strawberries on an industrial scale, people either squat all day long or lie on their belly on a wooden platform with their heads and arms hanging off the end; it's particularly brutal agricultural work. For me to go into the yard to pick a few berries for breakfast is a treat; for someone to have to pick them for 12 hours a day is torture. So the strawberry farmers, who already had some bad years thanks to unseasonable rains, started selling plants instead. The City even sponsors the Great Berry Bonanza each year to encourage people to grow their own. They're easy to propagate and anyone with even a patio or deck can grow enough for a household—all summer long with the ever-bearing varieties. Anyone eligible for Food Stamps can get a plant for free."

"What about people with Black Thumbs or who don't want to have a garden?"

"Remember all the kids selling them along the street Saturday? That's how people who don't grow their own can get fresh strawberries around here. Some people just set their excess produce out by the sidewalk with a Free sign."

The hills rolled this way and that, verdant with farms, fields and forest. Teresa downshifted to let a deer bound to the other side.

"One of my clients has scheduled their Barnstorm at the tulip fields today. So I finagled a way for us to join them. I assume we'll be digging the bulbs, but don't worry, there are lots of other things to do."

As they turned into the farm Joe noticed, beyond the fields, a stunning view of Mt. Hood. Teresa pointed at the mural painted on the side of the barn. It was the same scene but instead of rows of dirt and browning tulip leaves were vibrant ribbons of red, yellow, orange, and purple that undulated to the horizon. Joe was astounded. He'd never seen anything this beautiful that blended natural and manmade landscapes.

"Too bad it's not spring. It really looks like that. When we go inside, take a look at the posters. I try to come to their big festival each year, when the fields are in full bloom."

"It must be breath-taking," Joe whispered.

"Yeah," said Teresa. "Most of our farmland grows food for our stomachs or fuel for our cars, but this place is food for the soul."

After the orientation, Teresa headed to the fields with a garden fork, while Joe, to protect his aching back, sat in the shade of the warehouse, packing bulbs for next season. They were divided into teams of three. One person counted out the bulbs, another packed them with sawdust in a vented bag, and a third stapled on the tag with a picture of the flower and planting instructions. Periodically, these sets of bulbs were gathered up into flat cartons, which would be stored until fall when they would be shipped to stores. Since the work didn't require a lot of concentration, Joe struck up a conversation with his fellow 'day-laborers,' as he thought of them.

All the volunteers that day were from Pacific Natural Gas, the local gas utility. Ollie—who had owlish round glasses, an oddity thanks to the prevalence of laser surgery—was a policy analyst. *Whatever that is,* thought Joe. It sounded like a bureaucrat in disguise. Ann was a young, boxy woman who installed new service to homes. Joe figured from her short haircut she might be a lesbian, but what did he care. That sort of thing never bothered him. The owners of the farm rotated amongst all the tables making sure people were doing the job properly and replenishing their supply of bulbs. Their table was responsible for packing the spectacular Red Riding Hood tulips, which according to the packets, grew two feet tall and were a stunning Oriental red with black and yellow centers.

Joe started the conversation by explaining that he wasn't with the company but was here because of Teresa. Tess. He had to remember to call her that around other people.

Ollie brightened. "You're Tess's father? Waytago. She's been great to work with and a really big help."

Ann, who spent most of her time in the field, was less tuned into the stuff that went on in headquarters. The Ivory Palace was what her crew called it. "She was the one that did that sustainability training, right?"

"Yeah. She did that but she also helped us develop a whole strategy. We were so much in denial, hardly anyone wanted to think about sustainability. But then we got a new CEO who was fully on board."

Ann jumped in. "We—myself and the whole crew—thought he was nuts! Here we are, a gas utility. Natural gas. We make greenhouse gases for a living, right?" Joe gave her a confused look. "You know, natural gas, methane, a greenhouse gas. That's our product. At least the electric utilities had wind power. What were we going to do? I couldn't figure out how he thought bringing up climate change was going to help our business." She laughed hoarsely. "I almost started looking for another line of work!"

"So what happened?" Joe wanted to know. He could certainly empathize with their dilemma. Their whole business model was unsustainable. How do you work your way out of that? he wondered.

"So as you might imagine," Ollie explained, "we had a bunch of tough issues. How could we transition to something sustainable? What would that future look like? And how do we get from here to there without alienating employees and customers or putting ourselves out of business?"

Ann wagged a bulb in Ollie's direction. "But you did something, Ollie, that really helped me in that big meeting at the Tower. You reminded us how much our business had changed over the years. Originally we didn't sell gas at all; we sold appliances. Heck, before we had pipes all over the West, we made natural gas from coal and oil. So all of a sudden, talking about another major shift in our business didn't seem so impossible or unthinkable anymore. I still couldn't see where you were taking us with this but I at least had hope that if we could envision a future, we could do it."

Ollie gathered up an armload of bulb packets and counted them out as he put them into the carton. Joe tallied the inventory as the owners had shown them. One of the owners brought them large sacks for storing the remaining bulbs, which they would hang in the barn until fall and then replant the bulbs in a new location. Then they started on another variety, salmon-colored with what looked to Joe like shredded edges.

"Okay, I'm on the edge of my seat here. I can see you were in a box. You sold greenhouse gases for a living, as Ann put it, and after the success of The Inconvenient Truth, it was hard to just ignore that anymore. But what could you do?"

"That's where Tess was so helpful. She encouraged us to think about strategies for different timeframes. She worked with our executives to envision several possible future scenarios in which we could be fully sustainable, leveraging our physical and knowledge assets. That was an experience! All of a sudden, this 'undiscussable' issue became this exciting catalyst for new ideas."

"Like what?" Joe asked as he put a handful of sawdust into the bag of bulbs.

"We started to realize that our asset wasn't really the gas. Heck, we didn't produce most of that ourselves anyway. What we owned was a delivery mechanism. We had all these pipes to people's homes and businesses."

"So…?" Joe said, still not seeing a business opportunity.

Ann joked, "Well, we could tell you but then we'd have to kill you."

Ollie chuckled. "I don't think it's a secret anymore. It's in our Sustainability Report. One scenario relates to the hydrogen economy. If that finally takes off, our pipes can carry natural gas enriched with extra hydrogen. Fuel cells would provide both electricity and heat to homes, as well as pure drinking water. Without taking over an electric utility, we could in effect become one. Eventually to carry 100 percent hydrogen, we'd have to line the pipes with something to prevent the gas from escaping—the molecule is so small, it leaks out of practically everything—but this is a viable interim business model."

Ann jumped in. "And with this, we could not only put in the pipes but also maintain the fuel cells. So my crew isn't out of work; we'd have *more* work."

Joe was getting drawn into the excitement for a moment. "Maybe you lease the fuel cells, since front-end cost is such a barrier for homeowners."

Ann laughed, "That would put us back in the appliance business again, where we started 100 years ago."

"Okay," Joe said, coming back to present-day reality. "But the stock market isn't going to wait for the hydrogen economy to come along. That's taking longer than anyone thought. You'd get brutalized by the investment analysts if that were your whole strategy. What do you do in the interim to maintain your competitiveness in the marketplace?"

"That's been a little tricky," acknowledged Ollie, "but mostly from a messaging standpoint. We realized that we could still claim an advantage because natural gas can be used at the point where it's needed, so it generates less greenhouse gases for the work performed than electricity, unless of course, you're buying 100 percent green power."

"Why is that?" Joe wondered.

"Think about how inefficient centralized power plants are. They dig up a mountain to get coal or pump natural gas. Then a large percentage of the power goes to running the plant itself, perhaps 40%. And there's all this waste heat. Have you ever been in a thermal plant?"

Joe shook his head.

"I used to work for an electric utility years ago and I visited one. Ohmygosh, it was worse than the hottest sauna you've ever been in. Workers used to go up on the catwalks to kill off colds. It burned the inside of your nose, it was so hot. And instead of using that heat for something, they just vented it as best they could to cool off the place."

Ann explained, "I've read that in Europe, they've done a much better job of having combined heat and power plants where the heat is used to heat homes or power industry. But in the US, all the old power plants are in the middle of nowhere."

Ollie took back the conversation. "Then there are line losses. So, for certain applications, only distributed electrical generation, small units like in Tess's neighborhood, can compete with natural gas."

"That's really slick," said Joe. "You have a long term strategy to migrate to a new, clean-tech business, which is a great growth industry, as I'm sure you know. But in the meantime, you think you can steal business from your competitors on a cost, efficiency *and* climate perspective. Are people really going to buy this line of reasoning? Isn't this a little complicated to explain?"

Ollie nodded, "Well, as I said, it's a little tricky. We don't want the environmentalists among us to think we're spinning anything because that'll bring them down on us with posters and protesters. But we can do the math and explain the premise. And if you look at our profits and stock price, it seems to be working."

"So what does packing tulips have to do with all this? Your company gives you time off to do this?"

"Oh, that," said Ann. "It's better than crawling around in the mud putting in pipe."

Ollie smirked at her and then turned back to Joe. "It's just part of what we do to be good corporate citizens. We pick a different farm each year."

"But why farming? Why not something closer to your business?"

Ollie smiled. "We all need to eat, right? This started when farmers had more and more problems getting people to work in the fields."

Ann interrupted. From running a blue-collar crew, she had developed a dim view of work ethic of much of the American workforce. "The crackdown on illegal immigration blocked a lot of the hardworking Hispanics, and Americans are too lazy to do it."

"At a policy level, we started to realize that if the work really was that hard, perhaps it wasn't fair to make poor immigrants—legal or otherwise—do it. It really helped when the Oregon Legislature passed the tax deduction for volunteering. You can earn from $100 to $1000 off your taxes if you volunteer with an approved charity in the State, based on the number of hours you work."

Ann added, "And poor people who don't pay taxes can get the same amount in coupons good at the farmers markets, which comes back around to help the farmers again."

Joe recognized the rainforest economy at work again but didn't bother to bring it up.

Ollie nodded. "Since we're doing this on paid company time, the company gets the deduction for each of us."

"But a farm is a business, not a charity."

"Yeah, but it didn't take the farmers long to create a non-profit to coordinate this. Since food and biofuels are so important, most of the legislature was all in favor of this."

"This seems rife for tax evasion. Aren't people just downloading the Nature Conservancy logo and printing up fake documents to get the tax credit?"

Ollie snorted. "Hey, not a bad idea. But the charities are the ones that report the activity and they issue a form like a 1099 but with a negative number. It's easier to police the charities and they know if they falsify the data, they'll get pulled off the approved list."

Joe gathered up another armful of tulip packets and Ann counted them as she put them into the carton. "Teresa—I mean Tess—told me that some companies use these outings as training exercises."

Ann wrinkled her nose. "My friend, her company used it to teach quality control. I think that's a great way to take the fun out of it."

Ollie said, "My wife's company does this instead of a company picnic and I'm grateful for that. Those used to be deadly. I used to feel so uncomfortable talking to these people I didn't know. But these Barnstorms give us all something to do together which helps break the ice and it takes the pressure off of having to make so much small talk. We bring our kids sometimes too. This has helped them learn where food comes from and how much work it takes to get it to our table. They look at peas differently."

Chapter 9: Investing for the Future

The next morning, as they took Riga on his morning constitutional, Joe and Tess came across Emily picking berries in her front yard. Luckily for Riga, he'd already peed on a tree because the conversation went on longer than any anticipated.

Tess wasn't sure her motives were pure but she asked anyway. "Emily, since you teach Finance and Economics, I'm hoping you can settle a dispute we've been having."

Emily eyed each of them warily and answered, "I don't think I want to get in the middle of this."

Tess persisted anyway. "Dad, here, thinks that the only purpose of investing is to make money, the more the merrier, such that it doesn't matter what you own. With peaking oil supplies and rising prices, he continues to make a fortune off Exxon, for example, which I've told him to sell on moral grounds. From his perspective, it doesn't matter if he owns Exxon or BP. He'll take the one that he thinks will earn the greatest return."

"Ah," Emily pondered with a glint of humor in her eye. "An amoral investor. A rare species around here anymore. I think its primary habitat is Manhattan."

Tess put her hands on her hips. "So I told him owning companies like Exxon is like pimping." Emily laughed explosively and then quickly tried to put on a neutral expression again, but her eyes still sparkled with amusement. "He's making money off of other people's immoral acts. As you know, Exxon tried for years to obscure the truth about climate change until the effects were obvious to everyone. Instead of investing in research like BP, they spent money on a disinformation campaign. Then there's the mess associated with the Valdez. Whole communities have been ruined or moved and Exxon still hasn't paid a cent to some of those people. And there a workers with terrible medical conditions because they botched the clean up. The ecosystem there may never recover."

Emily held up her hand to stop Tess's torrent of complaints. "It seems that both of you assume that you have to earn less to invest in responsible or sustainable companies. You know that that isn't true, right? The Domini Sustainability Index has basically tracked the S&P 500, sometimes doing little better, sometimes lagging a bit."

"I told him that but he doesn't want to be limited. He wants to do better than the market."

"Can I get a word in edgewise here?" Joe asked, holding his hand up like a student. "Part of my argument is that unless you buy an initial offering, the company doesn't get the money anyway. I, in effect, bought the shares from someone else. So we're just trading money amongst investors, so what difference does it make?"

"It's true," answered Emily, "that the money doesn't go directly to funding the company operation. But you also have to acknowledge that, by trading the stock, you support their bond ratings, saving them money by keeping their interest rates down. And most of the executives probably own stock and options, so your investments enrich them personally by supporting the stock price."

"I hadn't thought of that," Joe answered.

"So do I win the argument?" It even sounded childish to Tess as soon as she said it.

Emily eyed her carefully, trying to discern the subtext to her question. "Tess, I said I didn't want to take sides. You also need to acknowledge that BP still puts at least as much money into extracting more oil as they do renewables like solar. And remember the spills in Alaska because they hadn't been maintaining their pipes? And that refinery explosion? They have some things to be embarrassed about too. This transition is tough for businesses. They have sunk capital costs they need to recover. They have employees and pensions and stockholders. They can't just turn off the taps, stop making a profit, and pump money into R&D for the renewable economy that still seems to be eluding us."

Joe apparently wanted to be the peacemaker. "So we both have been a little simplistic in our thinking."

Emily added, "You know, clean-tech is something you both should be able to agree upon. It's been booming for a decade now and still has a ways to go."

Joe nodded. "Actually, Teresa put me on to that a number of years ago. It's been a great play. As oil prices, the real estate bubble, and consumer debt walloped the market, it's been a tough number of years, but clean-tech has held up a lot better than the rest of the market."

Tess was astounded. "You actually listened to me and acted on it? Wow."

"You bet. And I and a lot of my clients should be grateful."

"Yeah, but you just wanted to buy it because it would make you money, not because it was the right thing to do."

Emily jumped in before they started on Round 2. "And we can all be grateful that the market forces and the environmental needs seem to finally be aligned."

Riga grabbed his leash in his teeth and backed up tugging. Tess laughed. "Well, on that note, I guess we need to leave now. Riga wants to walk and we need to go check on Rufus. Thanks for being our arbitrator."

Emily yelled after them as they took off down the street. "Mediator, not arbitrator. I didn't take sides, remember?"

On the way home, with Rufus and Riga vying for the lead, Joe asked, "You know what you've been saying about the toxics?"

"Mmm."

"Do you think that's what happened to Carol, her breast cancer?"

Tess sighed. "There's no way to know for sure, Dad. According to what I've learned from Mark, pinpointing the source of cancer can be very hard. We have lots of exposures to different chemicals all our lives. Some people are more genetically susceptible than others. What we do know is that many of these chemicals are carcinogens. Many mess with our hormones, which control so many processes in our bodies.

Many of these chemicals accumulate in fat cells like breast tissue."

"But up until the obesity epidemic, our life spans were increasing. If all these chemicals are so bad, why is that the case?"

"You may have also noticed that healthcare costs have skyrocketed too. The media likes to tout statistics about improved *survival* rates. What they don't say is that many cancer rates are also increasing. Years ago one in 20 women got breast cancer. Now it's closer to one in 8, although with fewer women using hormone replacement therapy, it dropped a bit."

"But isn't that rise in cancer rates a function of improved screening and longer life spans?"

"According to what Mark says, I'm sure some of it is from improved mammograms. But the top cancers in the US are in the prostate and breast. Testicular cancer is on the rise too. Those are all sites that concentrate hormones. It makes you wonder. Women can choose to stop taking HRT, but we can't stop absorbing all the other hormone-mimicking chemicals in use today. Women's breast milk is filled with synthetic chemicals. Orcas, which are high on the food chain, often give their babies such a high dose, their first calves die."

"I guess we aren't the only mammals on the planet, are we? Can you imagine trying to give an Orca a mammogram?" He snorted with amusement from the image it formed in his mind but then became serious again. "So we need the Race for Prevention instead of the Race for the Cure, for ourselves and other creatures."

"You bet. And not to start up the earlier argument again, but you know gasoline is a major source of benzene and it is one of the most carcinogenic chemicals we know. So if you want a personal reason to invest in a company that's trying to move away from petroleum, you could consider that. Everything is connected. Everything spreads."

Joe surprised her when he didn't have a retort. "How do you know all this stuff?" He sounded impressed.

"You remember how much I enjoyed science, even though you pushed me to study business." She still felt a little resentful—her father had thought she couldn't make enough as a scientist—but there was no point in reopening that wound too. "At least I found a way to combine the two," she added in a cheerier tone. They walked past the next house in silence.

"You know, you've mentioned Mark several times since I've been here. Do I get to meet this guy or are you hiding him from me?" He paused and then turned to look at her. "Or *protecting* him from me?"

Tess tried to chuckle but her stomach lurched. She knew how Joe felt about 'bureaucrats.' He was cynical and openly derisive about government in general. They were all, in his mind, louses or idiots or both. Furthermore, she was conflicted about her relationship with Mark. He was a wonderful guy and he kept asking her to marry him. But watching her parents' relationship buffeted against the rocks of life and seeing so many other marriages end in separate life-rafts kept her from diving in. And this reluctance had turned their relationship into an on-again off-again affair. She wasn't sure it was worth putting everyone through the meet-your-future-in-laws face-off if the relationship wasn't going to last.

She sighed. Since Joe had opened up to her at the Farmers Market, she decided to be honest. "Maybe a little of both." She really didn't want to explain herself even though her father gave her the opening by raising his eyebrows. He'd have a conniption if he knew Mark had asked her to marry him. "Anyway, he took the bullet train to Seattle for a meeting. He'll be back in a couple days. Maybe we could have dinner or something." She paused. "So I have a few days to work up my courage."

Joe reached across her back as they walked and hugged her shoulder, pulling her to him for just an instant before he let her go. She figured it was supposed to be an act of encouragement, but his attempt at chumminess felt decidedly awkward.

Chapter 10: Time and Money

Joe had been mulling the amount of time that Teresa seemed to have available. At first, he thought she'd just taken time off to be with him, but then he realized that she probably didn't ever work full-time. *How was the kid going to get ahead if she didn't apply herself?* he wondered. To get out of the tiny CCP, Joe had gotten in the habit of having breakfast in her sunroom, an informal space that grew vegetables all winter and heated her house in the spring and fall. When Teresa joined him with a bowl of cereal piled with fresh strawberries, he opened the conversation gingerly.

"It's been fun the last few days. How do you find the time to do all this? You seem able to drop everything to go visit Martha in the hospital or take the dog on a walk." He paused, trying to find a way to put this so it wouldn't make her angry. Finally, he had it. "Did you clear most of your calendar for me? I'm concerned that I am costing you a fortune in lost business."

Teresa smiled. "It's okay. I did postpone a couple meetings. But I don't usually work a full 40 hour week."

Forty-hour week! Joe thought. *That's a joke; who works that?* Everyone he knew worked 60-80 hours. Now he was alarmed. She'd been working to build this business for six years now and she still couldn't get enough clients to keep busy? Maybe this was the time to pop the question about going into business with him. How could he create an opening to bring that up?

"Honey, are you having trouble making this a viable business? You've been at it for years. Maybe it's time to think about doing something else." Ha, he'd done it. A perfect entrée to the reason for his trip. But her answer stunned him.

Teresa just shook her head. "You still don't get it, do you? I don't want to be a workaholic like you. I want to have time for my friends," she gestured toward him, "my family, and myself." She grabbed an envelope off the wicker table and a pen. "You always say, 'Numbers don't lie,' right? So let's do the numbers. I don't have to work as much because I don't need as much, and that makes it possible to have a balanced life."

Joe started a retort but Teresa held up her hand. "Humor me, okay. I want to do the math with you. Time is money, right? So let's look at the expenses you have that I don't and then let's look at the time I have that you don't."

She started a list. "So, first of all, I don't have a car. What's an average car payment these days, $400? Help me here. You're good at mental math. How much is that in a year?" Joe answered and she wrote down $4800. "Next, I build exercise into my day so I don't need a gym membership. How much is yours a year?"

And so the conversation went. Joe played along because he needed to understand her thinking before he could change her mind. It was just the same with his clients. After a short period of time, Teresa had created the following list:

	Dad's expenses I don't have	My expenses that Dad doesn't have
Transportation costs		
Car payments	$4,800	
Car insurance	$400	
Fuel (15000 miles at 30 MPG and $8 gas)	$4,000	
Repairs & maintenance	$300	
Zipcar		$2,000
Public transportation		$400
Housing		
Additional interest on mortgage for your large house	$5,000	
Additional maintenance, furnishings for large house	$200	
Sewer & water bills because you don't have bioswale and rain collection	$500	
Additional energy costs—from larger house and higher fossil fuel prices	$500	
Weekly garbage collection for Dad versus once a month recycling	$300	
Misc		
Extra groceries vs growing some of my own food	$1,200	
Unnecessary techno-toys (satellite TV, etc.)	$1,200	
Tools you buy because you don't have a Tool Lending Library	$200	
Beaumont Bucks to pay for tools and equipment		$40
Gym membership (amortizing the initiation fee over 5 years)	$1,500	
TOTAL	$20,100	$2,440

"So, your lifestyle requires you to make close to $18,000 per year more than me, just with these items alone."

"But," said Joe.

Teresa cut him off. "That may not sound like much to you, but over 10 years, that's almost $180,000 I don't have to earn. What's the average income for Americans these days?"

Joe didn't see where she was going with this but answered anyway. "I think around $50,000."

"So the average person could take a three-year sabbatical every ten years and still have a pile of money to go back to school or take a nice trip. Even a highly-paid professional could take six months or a year off every decade. And that doesn't count not having kids, which I understand cost close to

$400,000 *each* to raise to age 17, and then you still have to pay for college. But who knows, I might want to adopt someday. So I left that out."

Joe was stunned. The bit about the sabbatical was intriguing but he was distracted by her thoughts about kids. Wasn't he ever going to have grandchildren? Kids with his genes? Then, all of a sudden, he was worried about her 'plumbing.' "Adopt? Why not have your own?"

"Dad," she said in the exasperated tone of a teenager, "there are 7.5 billion people on the planet. The last thing we need is another one! There are so many children that still need good homes."

She pointed back at the envelope, clearly wanting to get back to that conversation, not babies. "Anyway, so we looked at the money side. Now let's look at time. You used to work about how many hours a week on average?"

Joe still wanted to talk about Teresa's thoughts about parenthood, but he played along again. "Sixty, give or take."

"Okay, you average sixty and I average 35, on purpose, mind you." She subtracted the numbers on a corner of the envelope that didn't have scribbles all over it. "And I rarely have to commute so that saves me an additional 7.5 hours a week. So I have 32.5 extra hours per week. If you leave out 8 hours for sleeping, that's like having an extra weekend *every* week. What would it be worth to you, to your family, to your community, to have an extra two days a week?" Joe didn't have an answer. He was still trying to imagine a life like that. Having *one* full weekend would have been a new experience. Joe had always had the Wall Street ticker scrolling along the top of his home computer and was the type to check his Blackberry on his bedside table.

"*That's* how I have time to spend with you, work in my garden, go see Martha in the hospital, and take the dogs to the park."

What happened to that great entrée to talk about Teresa coming to work with him? It seemed the moment had evaporated once again. Damn! *Oh well,* he thought. *I still have a few more days before I leave.* The thought of going 'home,' to that big empty house, made him melancholy. Somehow, in just about a week, Beaumont felt more like home than the place he'd lived for 25 years. Since he didn't want to deal with his feelings, he focused back on Teresa. There was something that still wasn't right.

Teresa had misinterpreted the wan expression on Joe's face. "Dad, you look so disappointed in me."

"Oh, honey, no, I'm not. I was just thinking about something else for a second." That's odd, thought Joe. A week ago, if she had told him all this, he would have considered her lazy, lacking initiative, living the selfish life of a hippie throwback. But he didn't see it that way anymore. He'd heard from the gas company employees how much she'd helped them. It was clear the same was true for her neighbors. She was playing a small part in a critical worldwide movement to transform our society. On the plane, he'd told that woman that he wasn't proud about her career. Now he wondered why. Other than being mad at him half the time, she seemed happy, fulfilled, at peace. But something still niggled him.

"Then what is it?" she asked, testy.

"I can see advantages to your lifestyle, now that you put it in black and white." He gestured toward the figures on the envelope. "I think the woman I sat next to on the plane was trying to help me understand some of this, that money isn't everything."

"Dad," she said with a huff, "money's everything to you. You were always working."

Had he really spoiled her so much that she didn't realize how fortunate she had been? "Just how else do you think we could pay for the house, for your mother's shopping trips, for our vacations?"

"You even worked through half of those!" she shot back.

"I had to! You still don't get it. Money doesn't grow on trees, you know."

She interrupted, "You say you had to, but you didn't. I didn't want all that stuff. I wanted you."

Joe was stunned. "You *had* me. I worked hard to protect you. You've never wanted for anything."

"Neither have you."

He'd hidden his past from her the way a parent shields the eyes of a child at a gruesome accident. Maybe this was time to tell her the truth. "That's where you're wrong, Teresa." She looked shocked, her eyebrows like two birds in flight. "You never knew your grandparents. They died before you were born, but I think they worked themselves to death, for me, to give me a better life. I can still remember going to bed hungry. During the occupation, life was really hard. My mom would look through the garbage for food for us. Then, when we came to America, my father couldn't do engineering work anymore because he couldn't speak English well. So he worked two jobs—a janitor and a taxi driver—so I could go to school. I swore to myself that my family would never have to eat from a trashcan, that I would make enough to send you to college. That's what the father is supposed to do, to sacrifice for his family."

Teresa clearly wasn't ready to give in. "And instead you sacrificed your family. You weren't there for me when I was a child and you weren't there for Mom..." She couldn't finish the sentence.

"I wasn't there for Mom what? What are you implying? I loved your mother."

"Not enough to stay home with her."

Joe's jaw dropped. "My God, is that what this is about? Are you still angry I wasn't there when she died?"

"You bet I am. How could you? How could you leave her alone like that?" She spat the words. "You chose to be with a client instead of her!"

"Do you think I wanted to?"

"No one forced you to go to that meeting."

He wanted to slap her. He'd never raised a hand to her but it was all he could do to control himself now.

He strained his words through clenched teeth, his hand clamped around her wrist. "Listen here. I begged my boss for a leave of absence, but the company wouldn't let me keep my medical benefits. Your mom's illness would have wiped us out. I *had* to keep working. Can't you see that? I had to. To protect her and to protect you. All those years of working and saving up for your education...."

His voice trailed off and he let her go. The argument brought the whole nightmare back. He'd cared for Carol every night, cleaning up vomit, dealing with her despair, begging her to eat. He stuffed the irrational anger; how could she do this to him? Then he juggled his work schedule around the vagaries of the in-home caregivers. He lost 30 pounds right along with Carol, as she wasted away to a Halloween skeleton.

He looked directly at Teresa, the spitting image of Carol when she was healthy, and tears welled in his eyes. He looked down at his hands. "That day, that morning, she seemed better. She told me to go. She said her friend Kirsten was coming by shortly. She sat up in bed and asked me to kiss her. She hugged me and whispered thank you." Joe choked and swallowed hard. "I thought she was just thanking me for the kiss."

He forced himself to look at Teresa, trying to decide if he should tell her everything. "After I left, she took her medicine. All of it." He watched Teresa to see if she was understanding. "The nurse showed me the empty bottle." His voice was just a whisper now. "Hospice had just given me a new prescription of MS Contin." Teresa's mouth was the shape of an O, like a caroler on a Christmas card. "Kirsten wasn't coming over." Horror registered on Teresa's face. "I guess she didn't want to go on; she didn't want to be a burden." He couldn't say anymore. It was too awful, too shameful. Instead he let out a sob and buried his face in his hands.

Time yawed in the sea of truth. He was too humiliated to look up, afraid of what he would see on Teresa's face. Now she would hate him even more. He could hear her breathing and sense her stare. She must blame him. Why else would Carol have given up? It was his fault that she didn't have a desire to live. He should have done more to make her feel loved. The worst part was feeling relieved that she did it. She was in so much pain unless she was doped up. She was just a shell of herself. What a monster he must be to have felt that way: shocked, grief-stricken but still relieved. No wonder Teresa hated him. But finally, there were no more secrets. He let out a shuddered sigh.

Joe heard Teresa say his name, but it was so quiet he couldn't decipher the tone. Then he heard fabric rustling like she was rising to leave. A moment later, when he expected to hear the door close, he couldn't have been more surprised to feel her arms reach out to hold him. He clutched her to him as their tears mixed on his cheek.

■■■ ■

Later that evening over dinner, Joe decided to bring up the conversation about Teresa's career again. Their new adult-to-adult relationship demanded straight talk. He took a sip of wine to have time to organize his thoughts. "This morning, when we were talking about your work, I didn't have a chance to finish my thought. You've clearly got more balance in your life than I have had, and I think that's a good thing over all. There's still something I want you to think about, though. You've been working with a handful of clients, and clearly doing good work for them based on what I heard at the tulip farm. And you've been able to earn enough to have what you want."

When he paused, Teresa said, "It sounds like a 'but' coming up."

"Yes, there is. Two, actually *But*," Joe emphasized the word, "first, I think you need to refine your message, lighten up on the doom and gloom."

"I don't sound like that," Teresa protested. Joe arched one eyebrow. "Do I?"

"Maybe not to all your friends who think the same way, but the people who think like you are already on board. If you want to get the rest of the organizations going, you have to be able to speak their language. What's the bottom line business reason for doing that?"

"I try to talk about the business reasons, but fundamentally, I do feel it's a moral issue. Maybe you can help me with the delivery. I don't want to sound radical or judgmental. So, you said you had two 'buts.'"

"Yes, I did." Joe looked at her proudly. "I wonder if you've been thinking big enough, strategic enough. If all you do is work with clients you can get to on your bike or bus, there's only so much good you can do. You really believe in sustainability. You want to change the world, right?" Teresa nodded. "So how do you take this business of yours to the next level? No offense, Oregon's great, but it's kind of a backwater. For you to change the world, you're going to have to make a bigger impact than consulting with one local company at a time." Joe could hardly believe what he was saying. What happened to his plan to talk her into going into the investment business? Where was he taking this conversation? He had no idea where this was leading. But for once, he was focused on Teresa and what she wanted instead of himself. And that felt really good.

Teresa looked stunned. "I'm intrigued. Like what? What would I do?"

"I don't know the answer. I only have the nagging question. But maybe we can explore this together."

"I'd really like that, Dad. Maybe, with all your business experience and exposure to big companies, you could help me. I don't want to give up having the balance in my life or spend my life on airplanes. Too many greenhouse gases there."

"And a miserable existence," Joe added.

"But who knows, maybe there is a different strategy. It's been a little lonely being a sole proprietor. Maybe, if I partnered with others, I could be part of something larger. If you could help me find a way to have a bigger impact, that would be great!"

Joe's chest swelled with pride, so much so it almost hurt. Maybe, in some little way, he could still be her hero again.

Two hours later, after analyzing what was needed and brainstorming ideas, both were energized by the idea they'd generated. For Joe, the added bonus was that it would give them an opportunity to collaborate. If it worked, it would give him a reason to stay in touch, and it would give Joe a new career that built on the relationships he'd developed over the years. *Without violating that damn non-compete clause,* he thought. Maybe he didn't have to put his life on hold for a year after all.

"You know," Teresa said almost breathless with excitement, "We need to get Emily's reaction to this. She could be a real asset." She paused. "But no hitting on her in my presence, okay?"

Joe was surprised that Teresa would have noticed his attraction. He liked Emily but good heavens, he wasn't trying to bed her or anything. Suddenly, the tone of the conversation they'd had in Emily's front yard made a little more sense. "Teresa, I think Emily is a very interesting and attractive woman. But I promise," he held up his hand in the three-finger Boy Scout oath, hoping a little humor would diffuse the situation, "not to seduce her for a one-night stand during my short trip here—in your presence or not." Teresa didn't answer but it seemed to be enough for her. "For what it's worth, I've never been that kind of guy."

Chapter 11: Exploring the Commons

It was one of those days that give Portland a bad name. While the rest of the country was basking in summer weather, Portland was dank, dreary and drizzling. Tess couldn't have been more nervous if they'd been on the way to meet the Queen of England. Mark, who had gotten back from Seattle the day before, had invited them over for dinner at his flat in The Pearl, the posh downtown area of condos and shops, walking distance to his office. Tess thought it might have been better to meet at a restaurant in the hopes that the ambient noise would prevent him from hearing when her father inevitably insulted his profession. But Mark insisted. He loved to cook. *Oh, God, what would Dad think of that?* she fretted.

Tess chewed her lip as they waited in the bus shelter with a handful of strangers, the rain darkening her mood further. *Maybe a preemptive strike was justified in this situation,* she thought.

She could see the bus a number of blocks away. Time was running out. "Dad?"

"Hmm?" He looked over at her and almost burst out laughing. He squeezed her shoulder. "Come on, Honey. I'll be on my best behavior. Promise."

The bus was approaching rapidly, so they got ready to board. The large doors opened at the same level as the shelter, but only for about 15 seconds before it took off again. That was one way it got downtown as fast or faster than by car. "You better," she said. They stepped on and quickly took a seat. Unlike a typical bus, this one had a long row of seats along the sides of the bus with a wide aisle. During peak times, many people stood, rocking from the straps that hung above their heads. This allowed the reticulated buses to carry over 100 people.

They sat side by side so Tess turned her knees toward Joe. "Look, Dad. It's more than just being on your 'best behavior,' as you put it." *That could be as uncomfortable as your being rude.* "What I'd really like is for you to appreciate how important the work is that Mark and his colleagues do."

"So educate me," Joe responded, touching her knee. "I've already learned a lot from you, you know. I'm not such an old dog I can't learn a new trick."

Tess knew she couldn't be petulant. She needed to provide a logical explanation that would make sense to her father, a long-time Republican, who believed in free markets, capitalism, and individual freedom. "I know you think that government is inefficient and businesses are, right?"

He nodded. "Yeah, I'll admit that. Guilty as charged."

"And it can be. No question. There are certain things that business can do better, at less cost."

"I'm with you so far," he teased, both of them knowing she was basically parroting what he used to tell her all the time.

"But here's the deal. Government and business do different things; they have different roles in our society. If you want Nintendos and Big Mac's, invest in business. If you want clean air, good schools and the infrastructure business depends on, we need to invest in government. So paying taxes, in my view, is not something to be avoided at all cost. Taxes are the fees we pay to have the benefit of the services government provides."

She paused while the bus stopped and people shuffled about, getting on and off.

"And in many ways, those services are more important to our livability. What is it worth to you to feel safe in your neighborhood? That's public safety. What is it worth to be able to easily get from one part of the city to another? That's transportation planning. Just think about the impacts that urban planning has. It affects whether you can get what you need easily, perhaps even without getting in a car. That affects both the air quality and your health, the amount of exercise you get. It even can affect whether you know your neighbors."

"How do you mean?" asked Joe.

"You know the busy street that the Butlers live on?" referring to some of his friends back home, a family that seemed to live in their car. Joe nodded. "It's not an accident they don't know any of their neighbors. They'd get run over if they tried to introduce themselves to someone across the street. The whole subdivision is made up of 'snout-houses' where the most prominent thing is the garage. You can drive in without ever having to say hi to neighbors on either side of you. The family room looks out on the backyard and there are no front porches, so no one ever sees anyone walking by. The street is so busy that no one, in their right mind, would let their kids play basketball in the street or even on the sidewalk. So the design prevents interaction. That's what I mean."

Joe nodded his head like he was mulling all this but Tess didn't think she'd scored yet. They were also getting close to the downtown area, crossing the Willamette River. So Tess tried to sum it up. "Government is responsible for the commons, those things that benefit us all, that aren't owned by anyone. The air, the water, the views, the streets, the parks. They are responsible for protecting us from crime, from fires, from toxins, from ecological collapse. Before Katrina, we also *thought* they were supposed to help us when the worst happens. When you think about the relative importance of what government is responsible for and business, which is more important to our well-being? We've developed this cynicism about government in this country, a chronic disrespect. But they have a critical role to play. That's not to say they always do it well; we need them to do it better. But they are the only institution that has the express mission to do what's right for the community. I guess that's the point I wanted to make." She glanced out the windshield beyond the driver. "Oh, this is our stop."

They walked in silence toward Mark's condo. In Joe's hometown, downtown was deserted at night; everyone went home. So he was fascinated to see all the street life. Small groups of people chattered away as they strolled the streets and headed into restaurants. Tess, on the other hand, could hear her heart pounding in her ears. *Why did it matter?* she wondered. Mark was just her boyfriend, right? Sure he'd asked her to marry him, but her father didn't know that. And she hadn't said yes. Yet. *Get a grip, Tess.*

To distract herself, she told Joe about the Living Building certification the condo had earned, a concept invented by architects in the Northwest as a simpler and more sustainable alternative to the LEED green building rating system. She explained that the complex had been built on a brownfield site. "It generates all the power it needs, at least on an annual basis, and it collects and treats all the water and waste water." She pointed toward a glass wall on the exterior of the building. "That trombe wall heats the building in the winter. It's like a skinny greenhouse on the south side of the building. And the rooftop garden attracts wildlife."

Tess made her father walk up the four flights of stairs to buy a little more time. Since Mark had inherited his Italian grandmother's love of cooking, the apartment smelled gloriously of garlic, onions, basil and tomatoes. When he opened the door, Mark gave Tess a quick kiss on the lips and then shook Joe's hand firmly. Tess could see they were both sizing one another up but guessed that was inevitable mano y mano behavior. Mark was about an inch shorter than her father, with dark wavy hair and a stocky build. The lasagna was about 20 minutes away from being ready so Mark offered them both a glass of wine.

The flat had the spare look of an industrial building converted to condos: tall ceilings, hard surfaces and a wall of windows with a view toward the river. But the walls were covered with large framed photographs of the city, waterfalls, mountains and rivers.

Tess gestured expansively, "Mark took all these."

Joe looked again with a more critical eye and was impressed. "You're quite good," he finally said.

Mark cocked his head. "You sound like you know a lot about photography. Do you do it too?"

Joe shook his head. "No, but when I was in school, I loved videography, so I have a little background in the visual arts."

"I didn't know that," Tess responded, amazed. "I can't believe you didn't mention that this morning. I can only remember you having a camcorder when I was very small."

She turned to Mark. "He has some embarrassing footage of me losing my bathing suit at the beach when I was five."

Mark chuckled. "Would love to see it some time." Then he addressed Joe. "So why didn't you pursue it?"

"Oh, I wasn't that good at it so I'd never be able to make a decent living at it. As Tess probably told you, I turned into a workaholic, so there was never any time."

"Well, I don't make anything doing this either," he said, gesturing around the room, "but I still enjoy it. It makes me see things more clearly, really focus. I can sit out on a ridge with a tripod for hours. It's very meditative, relaxing. Some guys fish. I shoot pictures." For the next ten minutes, Mark led Joe around to the various pictures, telling him about the subject and the lighting, while Joe commented on the composition. *Maybe he really is being on his best behavior,* Tess thought.

When they'd made it all around the apartment walls, Joe commented, "I had no idea Oregon was so varied! Back east, all we ever hear about are the trees and the rain. But you have deserts and sand dunes too. And that Columbia Gorge is really spectacular."

Tess said, "So you can see why I wanted to live here. We're an hour or two from the mountains, the ocean or the desert."

"Looking at this picture of downtown, I am reminded of something I noticed when Tess and I were walking over here. I didn't see any homeless people."

"That's 'cause we don't have them any more."

"What did you do, run them out of town?"

Mark smiled. "Oh we tried that in the old days. But they just moved to another part of town for a bit. No, actually, we discovered what should have been obvious. Homeless people need housing."

Tess cut in. "Duh." It sounded more childish than she intended so she started to explain. "The policy used to be that if you could show you were clean of drugs and alcohol and were trying to get a job, you'd be eligible for housing. Otherwise you had to take your chances at the shelters."

Mark picked it up from there. "But how can you get a job when you don't have an address or telephone number? If your life is a mess, not having a decent, safe place to stay just makes things worse."

Tess touched Mark's wrist. "I remember you telling me about these people who would get completely blitzed so that the shelters wouldn't put them out on the street in the middle of the night."

"Yeah, they used to release people based on how sober they were so it was actually a disincentive. If you were totally wasted, you got to stay in a warm bed all night."

Joe held out a finger as if to ask for permission to speak. "But isn't that rewarding anti-social behavior, to give derelicts housing?"

Mark started briefly but didn't take the bait. "Some people felt that way. But doing this seemed to help lots of problems. Pedestrians didn't have to feel guilty as they stepped around them. Businesses didn't have to worry about them scaring customers away. And I believe the data from social services indicates that a much larger percentage of these people are now employed than ever before. And it's easier to monitor those with mental illnesses to make sure they're taking their medicines."

"Remember, Dad, that the homeless are not just what you might think of as lazy drunks. Some are families on hard times, kids. The CCPs are one form of housing these people now have but there are other options as well, for ones that are really in tough shape, like with serious drug abuse problems. But the best part now is we finally have a 711 number."

"What's that?" Joe asked.

Mark answered. "Curitiba in Brazil, had this system for years. I don't know why we didn't have it sooner. There's now a free number to call if you see someone on the street who appears to need help. They dispatch a social worker and after a short diagnostic, they get them into the program that's most appropriate for them. The City just helps to coordinate all these non-profits. Some work with teenage run-aways, others with gangs, others with drug abuse, and so on."

The oven buzzer went off so Mark excused himself. Joe and Tess offered to help but he said to take their wine glasses to the table. A large wooden salad bowl brimmed with fresh greens. Mark brought out the steaming Pyrex dish of lasagna and went back for the garlic bread. Tess really appreciated all the effort he'd gone to on behalf of her father, especially since he'd just gotten back from Seattle. It couldn't have been easy to work all day, do the shopping, clean the apartment and then cook. "It looks and smells heavenly, Mark."

Tess tossed the greens with the dressing she knew was in the bottom of the bowl. Mark had taught her that this technique prevented the lettuce from wilting before it was served.

Joe took a bite of lasagna, expecting a meat dish instead of spinach. "Is everyone out here a vegetarian? I don't think I've eaten an ounce of red meat since I got here."

Mark shook his head. "A lot of people are but many just eat more of a Mediterranean diet. I'm not a strict vegetarian like Tess."

"Why do you do it, Teresa?"

She wiped her mouth with the cloth napkin. "It's healthier than the typical American diet, it costs less, it's better for the animals—most industrial livestock operations are cruel—and it's better for the environment."

"How so?"

Mark answered. "Lots of ways, really. It's inefficient to grow feed for livestock. With close to eight million people on the planet, it can be hard to justify growing eight pounds of grain to get one pound of beef when you could just eat the corn. Then there's the methane associated with cows, a greenhouse gas. They require lots of water, and the runoff from them can end up in rivers."

"The UN says that 18 percent of greenhouse gases worldwide are attributable to livestock; that's more than transportation and air travel combined! And did you know about 70 percent of our antibiotics are used on livestock? It's a major reason why we're getting resistant germs," Tess added.

"But you eat Emily's duck eggs."

"Yes, but they're treated well, don't have to die for me to eat, aren't loaded with drugs, and mostly forage for themselves, eating bugs and weeds in her backyard."

There was an awkward gap in the conversation. It made Tess uncomfortable, so even though Mark had just slipped a forkful of salad into his mouth, she asked him, "So how was your trip to Seattle?"

Mark's brown eyes sparkled as he held a finger up to his lips, indicating he needed a moment to chew. Finally he was able to answer. "That new bullet train is fantastic!" This was one of the projects the West Coast had used Obama's stimulous package for. He addressed Joe. "Normally, Amtrak took three-and-a-half or more hours to get up there. Because passenger trains had to yield to the freight trains, you never knew when you'd arrive."

"Just another symbol of our values in this country," Tess added, "making stuff more important than people."

"So how long did this new train take?" Joe wanted to know.

"I was up there in two hours. That's about half the time of driving. And it runs from San Francisco to Bellingham, mostly up the I-5 corridor. It took a huge amount of political will to get it done but now even the naysayers—well, most of them anyway—think it's worthwhile."

"So what was your meeting about?" Joe asked. *Here comes the interrogation,* thought Tess.

"Climate change, what else? It's still the biggest issue we have. We've made great strides through green building codes, waste reduction, public transportation and all. But that was the easy stuff. We're trying to put together a regional strategy to be climate neutral in 10 years."

Joe looked shocked. "Isn't that unrealistic?"

"What's the alternative? To poach the planet? It seems the West Coast often leads these efforts. Everyone else thinks we're nuts for a while and soon the rest of the country follows. So representatives from Oregon, Washington, Alaska, California and British Columbia were all meeting to come up with ideas for what could be done. We wanted something we could do to prove it was possible but also something that could be easily replicated elsewhere."

"Got any answers?" Tess wanted to know.

"Well, carbon credits, the cap and trade system, got us part way there. And it was effective because it helped to internalize the externalities."

Joe shook his head. "You lost me. Can you say that in English?"

"Sure. There are things that businesses include in their costs and things they don't, externalities. Before we had such a push for sustainable forestry, for example, a timber owner could cut his trees and sell them, covering the cost of bringing those trees to market plus a profit." Joe nodded his understanding. "But that timber owner *didn't* have to pay for the runoff from the clearcut that ended up in the stream which killed fish for the fisherman or clogged up the filters at the water filtration plant. And he didn't have to pay for the climate effects of no longer having trees soaking up carbon. Those are externalities, and business likes to push as many costs into that category to keep prices down."

"Uh, I think I got it."

"Okay, I have another one," said Tess. "Think about what nuclear power would cost if the utility had to include the cost of storing and protecting the nuclear waste for 10,000 years. That's a cost born by the Federal Government, in other words, you and me. But the utilities don't have to count that in their rates."

Mark jumped in. "So when people compared nuclear power to some other forms of generation, nukes might have looked economic, but not when you take into account the whole picture. That's life cycle costing."

Joe held out his plate for seconds and Mark loaded it up with more lasagna. "This is really excellent. It seems I've been eating more than normal but I got on Teresa's scale and I've still lost a couple pounds since I got here. Must be all the walking. Anyway, how are you going to deal with these *externalities*?" He said the word like it was a foreign language.

"Like I said, the carbon credits in effect increased the costs associated with generating greenhouse gases, but that didn't make enough of a difference for some products because the price is set by the market. So in other words, in some cases, the bad choice, the less sustainable one, may have still been the cheaper one."

"Ah," murmured Joe. "And most people won't pay extra for a 'green' option, despite what they say, right?"

"Right. So we want to institute a regional feebate system for products where this is a problem."

"Not another subsidy! That's just a tax in sheep's clothing," Joe responded, sounding disappointed in Mark for the first time that evening.

Tess thought, *Oh boy, here it comes. Round 1. Ding!*

"Well, depending upon which side you're on, it's a tax or an incentive. The way a feebate works is government imposes a fee on the less-sustainable options and then uses that fee to pay for rebates on the more sustainable options. So it's revenue-neutral. If, for example, electricity from coal is 10 percent cheaper than wind power, we can just impose a 10 percent fee on the coal plant and give the money to customers who buy wind power. Then wind power is cheaper. You know how much people used to drive around to save a penny per gallon of gas? All we have to do is make the sustainable choice a penny less than the traditional one. Presto! The markets work, but they work the way we want them to."

"I can see how that would get people to buy what you wanted them to, but I'm not sure how I feel about your manipulating the free market that way."

Well, at least he was tactful, Tess thought. She interrupted before Mark could answer because she thought she had an angle that Joe would respect. "*Emily* says there is no such thing as a free market, Dad. Our society imposes all sorts of restrictions. You're not allowed to make meth, even though there's a market for it. Smokestack industries and strip clubs usually aren't allowed to be sited next to schools. We don't allow unpasteurized cheese in this country, even though it tastes better. Markets are really good about allocating resources efficiently but they don't address fairness and they don't protect the commons."

To change the tenor of the conversation, Mark stood up and asked, "So..., anyone want strawberry-rhubarb pie?"

"Tell me you didn't make that too," said Joe in a tone that implied he didn't think Real Men baked pie.

"Nope. Picked it up at Whole Foods."

"Oh, my God, is this decadent," Tess said a few minutes later as she put one last mouthful of warm pie in her mouth. "When I brought up Emily earlier, I was reminded that we have some really exciting news." She glanced at her watch. "Oh, but it's going to have to wait. We better get home to Riga before he splits. I left him in the house because it was drizzling."

"Hey, you can't leave me hanging like that!"

"Sure I can," she said playfully, nudging Mark with her elbow.

"Women can be such a tease," Joe said, winking at him.

Tess huffed, "No seriously, this would take a longer conversation and I don't want to rush it. You still want to go hiking this weekend?"

"You bet."

"Good. We can talk then. I thought we could take Dad to Mirror Lake. It's not too long a hike—unlike the one you took me on last time—and it's got a great reward at the end."

"Sounds perfect. Why don't I pick you both up, along with Riga, of course, at 10 am on Saturday. I'll reserve the 'Petmobile' tonight to make sure we can get it. "

On the way back to the bus stop, Tess explained, "Zipcar didn't used to allow pets in their cars. But sort of like how, after Katrina, we learned you couldn't separate people and their pets. Zipcar finally had to give in and get a couple vehicles that could carry them. There are only a handful in this area, though, so it's smart to reserve early."

Chapter 12: Natural High

Riga adored the Petmobile. It was a symphony of scents that only he could decipher. It also —with the one exception of a visit to the Spay and Neuter Clinic—always meant a fun outing. So as Teresa let him out, he bolted toward the vehicle and jumped in as soon as Mark opened the van door.

Joe and Teresa threw their daypacks into the back. Joe noticed Mark's was a full-sized backpack and gave Teresa a questioning glance, feeling oddly under-dressed.

"That's Mark. He's always prepared. He probably has enough for us to live in a snow cave for a week. But I don't mind." She punched Mark's arm playfully. "The weight slows him down."

"Snow?" asked Joe, wondering if he needed a lot more layers.

Mark closed the rear hatch. "Don't worry, we're not going that high. It's all melted where we're going."

As they drove out of town, Joe could tell they were going east since the sun was in their eyes, already high above the mountains. In late June, the days were long. Once again, they quickly left the city and were in farmland, but here, Mt. Hood seemed an imposing force upon the land. Joe had always found volcanoes unnerving. He hoped Mt. Hood didn't pick today to erupt like Mt. St. Helens. They slowed as the highway wound through small towns.

"So when are you going to tell me the big news?" Mark asked as they hit a straight stretch of road.

"Later," Teresa said, "when we can sit down and talk."

Mark might have complained, but the road was beginning to wind around the mountain and he needed to concentrate on driving. The road was so steep that, for those coming in the reverse direction, there were steep emergency ramps of deep sand every few miles for runaway trucks or others whose breaks have failed. Joe didn't want to look at the steep drop-off to his right. He wished he'd sat on the other side of the car.

Joe felt like he'd been transported into one of those Honey I Shrunk the Kids movies set in a Lionel train set. The steep slopes dwarfed the 100-foot Douglas fir trees. Clear mountain streams gushed around boulders. In sheltered spots, there were even vestiges of the winter snows, drifts of road sand.

Mark finally pulled off the road into a Sno-Park area. Cars and semis still hurtled past them. Joe couldn't imagine why anyone would want to hike here. It was noisy. *And if one of those trucks loses their breaks, they'd scatter all these cars like bowling pins,* he thought, *flinging them into the abyss.*

Teresa handed him his pack and clipped a leash on Riga. She and Mark headed across a narrow bridge spanning the stream beside the parking area. Joe shrugged and followed. In the towering trees along the narrow trail, they fell into a rhythm. It was a steady uphill climb. Joe was grateful that he'd walked as much as he had recently or he'd have been hopelessly winded. But he was determined to keep up.

Periodically, Teresa would stop to point out a delicate flower or edible plant. Joe realized that within one or two bends in the trail, the road noise had disappeared, as if the trees smothered it in their boughs. Breathing hard, he started to notice the scents: damp earth and resinous evergreens. As the stiffness in his legs eased, he started to feel more vibrant, more virile. It was as if the strength of the volcano was seeping through his boots.

They traversed a long slope of talus, sharp rocks covering the slope both up and downhill from them. But instead of fearing it, Joe relished the sun that shone through the gap in the trees. After a steep set of switchbacks, they stopped for water. Riga, who was now off-leash, bounded back to wait for the next leg of their journey.

Joe welcomed the break but it didn't last long enough. It was harder going now. He stopped to peel off another layer of clothing, and he stuffed it in his pack. When he started up again, he had to concentrate so that his feet didn't stumble on rocks and roots. His former euphoria began to evaporate as the slope steepened and his muscles burned. Periodically he could hear Teresa and Mark talking but they were far enough up the trail that he couldn't make out the words. He was starting to wonder if he should just tell them to go on without him and pick him up on the way back, but Teresa yelled back, "Almost there."

When Joe got to the spot from which Teresa had called, he peaked through the trees and saw a lake. In the distance he could see Teresa standing by the edge. Riga bounded in and drank. Then he lay down in the water. *Thank heaven*, he thought. *Maybe we can stop.* They'd been hiking about an hour and the sweat trickled down his face. Teresa and Mark kept walking around the left side of the lake and Riga followed. He wanted to yell out, "Can't we just stay here?" but he didn't want to appear weak in Mark's eyes. So he trudged on.

After a few more minutes, Teresa and Mark stopped and removed their packs. Riga lay down to chew on the rawhide Mark gave him. Joe shuffled up to them. It felt like his pack was a pile driver, compressing him into the earth with each step.

"Turn around," Teresa said.

Joe swiveled on his heel to look across the lake that sat in a giant bowl of rock and trees. Suspended in the lake was the mirror image of Mt. Hood which, as his eyes looked up, towered over the next ridge. Instead of being intimidated, Joe was awed. It didn't look malevolent, just powerful, like a spiritual presence. The hairs stood up on the back of his neck like they had when his mother took him once to the old cathedral in downtown Riga. This place too deserved a pipe organ that could rumble your innards. There as here, rock and light defined the space. "Wow."

Mark nodded quietly and reached for Teresa's hand. "We love it here. There's something about this place. It's hard to put into words."

Joe nodded, grateful that Mark didn't expect him to explain the joy he felt bursting in his heart. A yellow butterfly landed in the mud in front of them, unfurling its long tongue to probe for minerals.

Without even taking his pack off, he plunked onto a rock and sat, speechless, looking over the scene. He watched as the remaining mist curled tendrils off the lake surface. He started to notice birdcalls that his ceaseless inner voice had been drowning out.

A bug-eyed dragonfly of iridescent turquoise landed on a reed. Maybe it was the old woman's book on the airplane that made Joe study it carefully. *How could something so delicate be so enduring?* he wondered. When it cocked its head, it seemed to Joe to ask, What are you doing here? Of course, there were two interpretations of that question, Joe realized: What are you doing here at my lake and what are you doing here on earth? There was something eerie about having one of the most ancient, well-adapted species pondering him in that way. In contrast, humans—at least those in Westernized, developed countries—seemed adaptable more than well-adapted. Here, the dragonfly barely bent the reed from which it hung but humans had stomped ecological footprints on every part of the globe and even in space.

Joe wiped the trickle of sweat from along his sideburn and the dragonfly took off. But the question remained. It was more complex, Joe realized, than he had first thought. It mattered which word you emphasized. He'd focused on the last word, what are you doing *here?* But it could also be, what are you *doing* here, emphasizing your actions and impacts; or what are *you* doing here, emphasizing your individual role and contribution; or *what are* you doing here, which seemed to question your right or suitability. Tone mattered too. The question could sound judgmental or inviting.

What must it be like to trace your ancestry back over 300 million years, a design so elegant it has survived asteroids and ice ages? By contrast, Homo sapiens seemed destined to snuff themselves out in little over 10,000 years.

Perhaps instead, Joe pondered, humans might be undergoing a slow metamorphosis similar to that of the dragonfly nymph. He felt he'd undergone a partial transformation in just a week. How long might it take for our civilization to transform into a higher life form? Could it be that Teresa's generation was the one to break free of the surface and soar amongst rainbows? How many more skins would we have to shed for society to be ready?

How differently they would look upon their past life— an existence that seemed like the only one possible at the time. After dancing on dewdrops in a shaft of sunlight, a return to the depths would be as unthinkable as the ascent seemed to us now.

Maybe then we will be able to see with multifaceted eyes, simultaneously processing our social, environmental and economic impacts of our choices. Perhaps we could hover or reverse direction with the same ease that we now hurtle forward in the name of 'progress.' Our biggest challenge would be to become an integral and useful part of our natural surroundings, instead of a greedy usurper.

They sat like three birds on a wire, soaking in the spectacle. For how long, Joe couldn't say. Maybe it was an instant. Maybe it was an hour. Joe could simultaneously feel the pulse in his bellybutton, hear the wind swirl through the trees, and feel the sun on his arms. And yet, he was so lost in the image of the mountain, it seemed to breathe with him. He could sense Mark and Teresa observing him out of the corner of their eyes, but he felt no pressure to stop doing nothing. *What a funny concept,* he thought, *to stop doing nothing.* Joe heard a couple other people pass behind them on the trail, and their chatter seemed sacrilegious.

Finally, Teresa broke the spell with a satisfied sigh. "I'm starving. Anyone want something to eat?" Riga, as usual, was first in line.

In the midst of mouthfuls of cheese, bread and dried fruit, Mark looked at Teresa intently and to start the big conversation, simply said, "So…?"

Teresa looked at Joe. Her smile warmed him like a hot cup of cocoa. "Ohmygosh, I almost don't know where to start. Dad the other day said something like if all I did was work with the clients around town, I'd only have a limited impact. He thought I should think bigger. The whole field of practice has changed so much, so many more organizations are pursuing sustainability now. My practice needs to evolve too. Yet in so many ways, most Americans really haven't changed how they live."

"I know I didn't get it," Joe said, wanting to be supportive. "When I heard Teresa talk about how she was living, it always sounded like such a sacrifice. We had so little as a kid that I thought money and stuff would make me happy. Frugality reminded me too much of growing up, when we truly didn't have enough. If Mom found an empty bottle on the road, it was a great find. Reusing was almost a matter of life and death for us. So I couldn't imagine why Teresa would want to do it voluntarily. But I can see now that moving toward a more sustainable lifestyle isn't about giving up things you care about; it's about getting more of things you really want in life: time, friends, community, peace of mind."

"So...?" Mark said again, eagerly awaiting the punch line.

"So," Teresa answered, "Dad and I spent part of a morning thinking about what was needed now to move our society forward and what I had to offer. Actually, what *we* have to offer." She smiled at Joe. "We came up with this idea. I don't know if it's going to fly but it's worth a try. I'm going to write a grant proposal to start a Public Broadcasting series on sustainability. Dad thinks he can line up some of his well-healed and well-connected ex-clients to put up the funding. And I did some work with Oregon Public Broadcasting, so I have some great contacts there."

"Gee," Mark said, his brow wrinkling. "This sounds really exciting. I don't want to be a wet blanket, but do you know anything about making TV shows?"

"No, I'll need to assemble a team. But I can be the behind-the-scenes expert."

"Why not you in front of the camera? Maybe Leonardo di Caprio and Bono will be too busy," Joe replied only half-joking, thinking that once again she was selling herself short.

"Oh, Dad. We'll have to see about that. The producer and director would have to decide if I'm suited. But at least I can identify the topics, pull in the speakers." She looked at Mark. "Between you and me, we know practically everyone in this field on the west coast."

"Maybe with one or two degrees of separation anyway," Mark agreed.

Teresa was starting to bubble with excitement. "There are so many shows out there about what's wrong. I want this to be about what's being done and what each person can do. Remember that PBS series on small business. Hattie Whatsherface interviewed different business people about how they managed their businesses. This could be the same sort of show. We could highlight different organizations. Success stories usually inspire others to follow."

"Or maybe the show needs to be focused on citizens and what they need to understand and change," Joe suggested.

"Maybe." said Teresa. "My connections might not be as good for that."

"I don't know, Sweety. You gave me quite an education in a short period of time. If you could just show the world how your neighborhood operates, I bet a lot of people would try to follow suit."

"Well," she looked at Mark. "You can see there are a lot of questions that have yet to be answered. We don't even know if this will get funded. It doesn't have to be full-time. I think it's even better if I can keep my consulting practice because it'll keep me up-to-date. That way, if it fails, I'll just crank up the consulting a bit more again."

Mark snorted. "I've yet to see you fail at something you put your mind to."

"So what do you think?"

Joe noticed she asked Mark a little nervously but also with deep respect.

Mark thought for a second. "Well, Tess, you've organized all sorts of other events with speakers and panels, so this probably isn't all that different. Like you said, it would need to be a team effort. And you certainly know your stuff when it comes to sustainability. You've earned the respect of people around here so I know you'd get support. The trick is going to be to get into these different markets. You don't want to just sing to the choir and OPB's market is largely that. You have to entice people who don't even know they need the show. I wonder if you need to go mainstream. I don't know how you get there from here—that would be much harder—but you need to get into places that don't already 'get it.'"

For an instant, Joe was angry with Mark for shooting down the idea. Or maybe he was angry with himself for not catching this flaw in the plan. But he couldn't fault the judgment. On second thought, Mark wasn't putting a stop to it; he was trying to redirect it. Joe was impressed with his analysis. "You know, you're right. This needs to be national. It can't be just an Oregon thing."

Teresa was crestfallen. "I thought we could produce the show here, but you're right, we can't be sure it would get picked up in other locations or how quickly. Damn. I was really getting excited. It would be much more difficult to get funding for a national show with my lack of experience."

They all sat there, mulling the dilemma, looking for answers in the depth of the lake. When it didn't provide one, Mark tried to pick up the mood. He kissed her cheek. "Don't give up. You're onto something here. We just don't quite know what it is yet."

She smiled wanly. "Thanks, Mark. You're always my biggest cheerleader. I appreciate it." He looked at her doubtfully. "Really." She glanced at her watch. "Hey, we'd better start back down soon if we're going to get to Emily's in time for dinner. Since this is Dad's last night, she offered to have us over, and I need to pick up some wine on the way home. You *sure* you can't come?"

Joe could tell that Mark felt torn by competing obligations. He knew the feeling well. What he didn't anticipate was the reason. "I promised to teach the neighbor kids how to tune up their bikes this evening. Tell you what. Tell Em I'll try to make it for dessert. We should be done by then. Okay?"

Joe watched Teresa brighten at the prospects of seeing him again. It left him in a pensive mood all the way back to the car.

Chapter 13: Sustainable Business

Later that evening, Joe and Tess showed up on Emily's doorstep with a bottle of wine and a salad filled with greens from her garden. Tess was pleased to hear her father's description of the hike when Emily asked about it. He'd looked whipped when he arrived at the lake, but that clearly hadn't affected his ability to appreciate the place. Joe had been quiet coming down too, but hiking single file made conversing a little tough anyway. And Tess liked the solitude of her thoughts and observations. Nevertheless, she was thrilled to hear Joe call Mt. Hood magnificent. They didn't have mountains like this back home.

Tess asked Emily about Trevor since she knew this was her day to visit. "He's home now, but he looks so weak!" She just shook her head.

A buzzer went off in the kitchen so Emily excused herself. She brought out a bubbling casserole, a Mexican dish of some sort, with black beans, tortillas, cheese and eggs, of course. As usual, it smelled delicious. Neighbors ate together so often that people didn't fix fancy food. The potluck custom did, on occasion, result in some odd food combinations such as, in this case, red wine and Mexican. Had Tess known what Emily was serving, she would have brought a six-pack of Full Sail instead.

As they all sat down at the table, Tess poured the wine, being careful not to drip any on the white, embroidered tablecloth that she knew Emily pulled out for special occasions. Mark had not yet arrived. She was about to tell Emily about the TV show dilemma when Joe tapped his glass with a knife.

"First, a toast. To family," he looked lovingly at Tess and then at Emily, "and friends. I can't thank you enough for making me feel so welcome. I guess it's probably not a secret that Teresa—Tess—and I...well, let's just say we hadn't talked much in a while. So I wasn't sure what kind of a reception I'd get." He held his glass up toward Tess, a gesture that brought a lump to her throat. "Thank you for letting me be part of your life for the last 10 days."

Tess just clinked her glass with his since she didn't trust herself to speak. She thought he was done but he started speaking again after a brief hesitation.

"Second, I have a confession to make." At first, Tess wondered if it might have to do with Emily. Who knows what he'd been up to when she was working. But Emily looked just as mystified. *Can't be that,* Tess thought. She took a bigger swig of wine, not knowing what to expect. Joe went on. "I originally came here to convince Tess to come home and start a brokerage firm with me."

Tess almost spewed a mouthful of red wine across Emily's nice tablecloth. While she struggled to swallow, Joe continued, "I know. It was asinine. And selfish." Emily, wisely, kept her thoughts to herself.

"Good grief, Dad," Tess sputtered. "I knew you were up to something that you were having trouble bringing up, but that! Could you really imagine me as an investment advisor?"

"Not now, no. You'd be good at it; don't get me wrong. But I can see it wouldn't make you happy. Nor would moving. It's like you've made your own little habitat here. I can see why you love it."

Emily finally ventured into the conversation, albeit gingerly. "I'm curious, Joe, what led you to want to do that given, by your own admission, you two weren't on the best of terms."

Joe sighed. "To be honest, I think I was desperate. Carol was gone. I'd lost my job. My so-called community is nothing like what you have here."

A torrent of emotions buffeted Tess: guilt, empathy, sadness, love. She struggled to contain her feelings as she reached across the table and touched her father's hand. "Oh,

Dad. I'm so sorry. I didn't know." She paused. "Maybe I didn't *want* to know."

The doorbell announced Marks' arrival. "Just in time for dessert, as promised," said Emily as she rose from the table. After Mark sat down, Emily brought out dishes of vanilla ice cream covered with warm peach cobbler and crystallized ginger.

"I froze these peaches last summer," Emily beamed. Groans of delight rolled like a wave around the table as everyone took their first bite.

"Oh, my God, Emily, this is the best ever," Mark offered.

"So I was just going to tell Emily about the box we find ourselves in," Tess said to bring Mark into the conversation. She turned to Emily. "Mark raised an issue I think we need to address. Actually there are two issues. First, I don't have any experience in TV. Maybe we can overcome that with the right team. But the second issue is that OPB isn't the right market. We need to get into the national market to help educate people who don't truly understand sustainability yet."

Mark added, "I've been thinking about national TV and what shows have been popular."

"Have they finally stopped those Machiavellian reality shows?" Emily wanted to know. She'd recycled her old television when it died around the time the country switched to digital and never bothered to replace it. She could watch anything she wanted on her computer, and there wasn't much she wanted to see.

"I think it's going to be key to name it something other than sustainability," Joe offered, "so that it attracts a full range of people. It seems like what you have here is a different lifestyle."

"Maybe we need the Lifestyles of the Rich and Infamous," joked Emily.

Tess wrinkled her nose. "I don't want to put people down."

"I know," Mark jumped in. "Maybe we need something like that Nanny 911 show or the one where they build a house in a week. You and a team go in to solve a sustainability problem. You redesign the work process or the household. We could call it Lifestyles 911."

"I think I could see that working," Emily said, trying to be encouraging. "Maybe you could engage college students to go in and do a sustainability assessment of homes or businesses. Tess, you could be one of a panel of judges to assess the recommendations and maybe they compete for funds to actually do the project."

"Now, there's a thought," Joe said, rubbing his chin. "My corporate clients, especially those with more sustainable products, might be very interested in backing that as a way to sell their products. That home building show was basically an infomercial for Sears and their other backers anyway."

Tess was nodding and scraping her bowl at the same time. "Maybe like CarTalk, we check back in six months later to find out if it worked."

"Radio!" Emily shouted. "Maybe it's not TV at all. What was that Twisted Sister show?"

Tess guffawed. "That's an old rock group. I think you mean…, oh, what was the name of that show?" She looked at Mark for answers.

Mark had a knack for bypassing a diversionary question and getting to the heart of the matter instead. "I think the problem here is we have too many good ideas," Mark said. "We can't do them all."

There was a lull in the conversation. The grandfather clock in the hall ticked away the time. The energy in the room nosedived.

Suddenly Joe looked like he'd had an epiphany. Everyone could sense his excitement because his expression was electric. "Mark, that's it! There *are* too many ideas. And why is that? It's because *we* can't do them all. And because there isn't enough funding. These ideas we've been kicking around are great, but maybe Tess isn't the right one to carry them out. But there *is* something we can do together that makes sense, that leverages the strengths we have. Why don't we start a sustainability business incubator?"

The idea was such a departure, everyone looked stunned. "Don't you see? This takes advantage of both of our assets. Organizations need knowledge and capital. Teresa, you consult with organizations to make them more effective. And I know lots of investors, many former executives, who might be willing to advise the new ventures. You know which existing ventures might be ripe for expansion. Maybe this TV show is one of the projects. But let's launch a hundred ventures, not just one."

The collective ah-ha moment caused a momentary silence and then catalyzed a flurry of conversation. They were all so excited, they talked over one another.

Tess said, "There must be a thousand people just in Portland who have great ideas who can't do them because they don't have the money or the knowledge or both."

Mark said, "This could be a great economic development strategy!"

Emily said, "A bunch of my students each semester have entrepreneurial ideas that wither because it seems too hard to get started. Maybe the college would host the incubator."

A geyser of ideas exploded to the surface and swirled together, pushing aside pebbles, pouring around boulders, forming a riverbed that directed the flow.

An hour later, it was dark outside and a bottle of brandy was half empty. Tess drained her glass. "Oh, my head is reeling! And I don't mean from the booze. What a stimulating evening! But Dad, you have to pack."

"Who are you flying?" Mark asked.

"Virgin. Why?"

"You know that air travel is one of the fastest growing sources of greenhouse gases, right?" Joe shrugged. "If you pay for carbon offsets, they'll let you board first, ahead of even first class."

"Really? That's a nice incentive. I'll do it when I print out my tickets tonight. Thanks!"

Tess stood up from the table. "Oh, Emily, thank you so much for having us over. But we really must go." As they gathered in her entrance, the parting hugs took on new significance.

"I hope you'll come back to visit," Emily said to Joe as he shook her hand.

Chapter 14: Considering Commitment

Joe had had a restless night. Maybe it was all the alcohol or the spicy food. He spent much of the night strategizing about their new venture. Once Teresa and he wrote up the business plan, he figured he'd have no trouble getting backers. He made a mental list of the investors he would approach. Joe had a lifetime of relationships that could help get this going.

But it was a different set of relationships that had had him tossing and turning. Over coffee the next morning, Joe was still debating whether to raise the issue of Mark with Teresa. He didn't want to spoil their last morning together. He scratched Riga behind the ears. "What do you think, Buddy?" His answer was as obscure as the marine fog that blanketed Portland.

Teresa came through the sunroom door. "You're up early. Think about what?"

Joe decided he might not have another chance. It was time to do his fatherly duty. "Have a seat. I want to talk to you about something."

"Sounds serious. Let me get my tea first." She left to clip a few leaves from her new lemon verbena plant in the kitchen window to add to her hot water. She was still smarting from Joe's comment about her addiction to coffee and was trying to break the habit. The tart scent was enlivening.

Joe hoped he could find the right words that would make her understand. In a moment she returned. When she sat down across from him, he took a deep breath. "You and Mark have been dating a long time."

"Yeah," she said guardedly, "off and on." She eyed him over the rim of her cup.

"So how do you feel about your relationship?"

Teresa clearly didn't want to answer. "Where's this going, Dad? I know how you feel about people in government. Are you afraid we're going to get married or something?"

"Actually, I'm afraid you won't, at least not for the right reasons."

Teresa was stunned, her jaw gaping.

"I know I haven't held government bureaucrats in high esteem, but I like Mark. He's sharp and he clearly adores you."

"How can you tell? Hey, I thought you said guys can't decipher emotions." Joe noticed that Teresa was still trying to derail the conversation.

"Oh, we can't, except in two situations: power and girls. Those we have nailed. Consider it an evolutionary necessity. We had to know if another guy liked a girl or we'd bash in all our heads with clubs and our species would come to an end." When Teresa laughed, Joe was pleased he could lighten the mood. But he still had some important things to say.

"Three years is a long time to date. I'm curious, has your relationship not progressed because you don't feel the same way, or what?"

Teresa sighed. "Oh, Dad. Mark's great. He's kind. Like you said, he's smart. I respect the work he does. I feel good and safe when I'm around him. We enjoy a lot of the same things."

"But...?"

"Okay, I've got a confession too." Teresa couldn't look at her father when she told him. "He *has* asked me to marry him, a couple times." Now it was Joe's turn to be surprised. "I keep telling him I'm not ready. That hurts his feelings and then we usually break up. But we keep coming back together. And then we go through the whole pattern again."

Joe forced himself to be silent to encourage her to talk.

"I guess I don't see the point these days. I'm not dying to have a kid. Maybe I'm afraid that getting married will ruin what we have."

"Sounds like *not* getting married could do that too." He paused to let that sink in. "Look, Teresa, you're a grown woman and maybe this is none of my business. But I really want you to be happy." Teresa looked like she was going to say she knew that, but Joe stopped her. "Please, let me get this out.

I've been thinking a lot since I got here and I've watched you and Mark together. Only the two of you can decide if you want to marry. But I want you to know I like him and you two seem to really be a good team together."

Joe scratched Riga's back, that itchy spot, and he shuddered with delight. "Look, Sweety. I know your mom and I probably weren't the best role models. We fought a lot. She wasn't always so angry, so materialistic. I think I made her that way. She thought she married me and I married my work. And she put her career on hold for years when you were young and never really caught up. She loved you and wanted to stay home while you were little but still it was hard. I think shopping helped build her self-esteem." He shook his head. "I had no idea so many things had brand names!"

He glanced at her to see how she'd react to that slip-up. He hadn't meant to say something unflattering about her mother.

Teresa's surprise turned into a snort. "Yeah, it wasn't just shoes and handbags. Remember the refrigerator? She was so mad when we didn't appreciate it. What was it called?" Now it almost seemed nostalgic, or tragic.

"Oh, God it was huge!"

"It was like something from the Jetsons."

"Oh, and remember the corkscrew!"

They both started giggling and laughing, one-upping each other with materialistic memories until they both wiped tears from their eyes.

"Anyway," Joe finally said, trying to get back on track, "looking back, I know we probably did a lot of things wrong. No marriages are perfect." He waited until he had eye contact. "But there is nothing like having a partner in life, someone you can count on, who you know wants the best for you, who will be there through thick and thin. I know I wasn't as available as I could have been, but I think Carol knew that I always loved her. When she was so sick, I still held her at night, trying to comfort her. Teresa, you have a strong community and wonderful friends, but a life partner is something much more. I just hope you can have that someday."

He set his cup down with an air of finality. "So marry Mark, or don't. But make the decision that's right for you, not because you fear I'll disapprove or because you're trying so hard not to be like your mom and me."

Tears glistened in her eyes. She rushed over and gave Joe a firm hug and he held her to him. He kissed her cheek hard, as if he were making up for all the missed opportunities of the last few years. And then he let her go. There, he'd done what he really came for; he just didn't know it at the time. He'd done what he could to get her on the right path. Not just her career; also in life. And in turn, he too had a new direction: to finance a business incubator that would expand the sustainable innovations already in use here as well as invent new ones.

Teresa sat next to him, cupping her tea thoughtfully. "Dad, if you're lonely, why don't you move out here?"

"I can't, at least not right now. I have too much to do back home. That's where all my contacts are. I can do more good to you there. Mind you, I'm not a complete convert yet. I still want my banana in the morning." They both laughed. "But maybe I can pass on some of what I've learned on this trip to people in my neighborhood." She looked disappointed. "We'll talk every week. I know you don't like technotoys, as you call them, but I'll send you an upgrade. The new big screen Skype with Cisco's TelePresence is really almost as good as being there. You'll be able to meet clients all over the globe without leaving your sofa!" He hugged her again and whispered in her ear, "But I can't tell you how much it means to have you ask."

He could see it so clearly now. Sustainability. Livability. Quality of life. They were one and the same. For the first time in his life, he had a calling, not just a career. *Better late than never,* he thought. He now knew what he could contribute to the well-being of the world. He would spend the rest of his life trying to help others answer the dragonfly's question.

What are you doing here?

Discussion Guide

This novella was written to impart important concepts about the choices our society faces. All of the innovations presented in this book are either already in practice somewhere in the world, are a logical extension of what is already happening somewhere, or have been found by an expert in the field to be plausible.

While this novella can just be read for pleasure, it will have the greatest effect if it is read and discussed as a group. To that end, I'm providing some brief background information and suggested discussion questions for each chapter. Whether you read this with a group or on your own, there is an action plan at the back of the book to keep notes of things you want to do differently at work or at home.

How to facilitate a discussion course

I recommend conducting this discussion course in 8 1.5-hour sessions where the first session is an introduction to the course and the remaining seven sessions cover two chapters at a time. If you only can meet for an hour, either cover one chapter per meeting or be selective about the questions you discuss. Many groups like to have access to the Internet during their meeting so they can look up information they are curious about.

Introductory session
- Have every person introduce themselves and explain why they wanted to participate in this discussion group.
- Explain the purpose of the discussion course and go over ground rules for participation. These may include:
  - Start and end on time.
  - Come prepared (read and think about the chapters).
  - Bring your whole self, not just your work personae.
  - Take this commitment to the team and yourself seriously; only miss a session in extreme circumstances.

- o Share responsibility for running the course (see roles below).
- o Other? (ask if people want to suggest other ground rules to make this fun and educational

- Hand out copies of *The Dragonfly's Question* to each person.
- Point out that the discussion questions are in the back of the book.
- Determine roles. Bring a sign-up sheet so that people can volunteer to facilitate or open one meeting. If your group is small, some may need to volunteer twice. I recommend rotating the responsibilities in each meeting:
  - o Facilitator—This person reviews the discussion questions in advance and plans how to conduct the session. He or she also sends a reminder to all participants about the upcoming meeting. He or she facilitates the meeting and if appropriate, summarizes any to-do's or commitments afterward.
  - o Opener—This person brings in something personal to share with the group, something that in some way symbolizes some aspect of sustainability to them. This can be something tangible (a piece of art, a tool, a photo, etc.) or some other offering (a short reading, a story, etc.).
- If necessary, set the dates and times to meet. (If you can, use Outlook or something like it to find times that work for everyone before the meeting. Otherwise, have people bring their calendars. You can mock up a large two-month calendar with AM and PM in each day. Then have people indicate the regular meetings when they would not be available. This can help you quickly find dates that work for most..)

Remaining sessions

The facilitator should welcome the group and bring the meeting to order.

- Turn the floor over to the Opener to share what they brought (5 min).
- Facilitate a discussion around the first of the two chapters covered in that session (25 min)

- Facilitate a discussion around the second of the two chapters (25 min)
- Close by summarizing themes and remind everyone of the date and time of the next meeting and the chapters they are to read. Also remind the facilitator and opener for the next meeting. (5 min)

Chapter 1: Resurrecting Rifts

Group exercise: The purpose of this exercise is to get in touch with heart-felt concerns and also understand the systemic connections between them. It builds trust because people talk about issues they care deeply about, creating a tone for your meetings of speaking from the heart. It also helps each person to see how their concerns relate to sustainability, how they relate to the triple bottom line: social, economic and environmental health.

Create a chart with three columns: Social, Economic, Environmental. Then ask each person to talk about a couple issues that most concern them that fall under any of the categories. Once everyone has listed their biggest concerns, discuss how these issues relate to one another, drawing lines between them.

Tess alludes to the greenhouse gases associated with air travel. But even if you must fly, there are ways to reduce the impacts. See the Union of Concerned Scientists' *Getting There Greener* website to learn more: www.ucsusa.org/gettingtheregreener.

Technology: Tess answers her i-All, what I imagined the next generation of the i-Phone might be, which in a later chapter, also communicates with her Smart House appliances. However there is little allusion to consumer electronics in the rest of the book.
- How has this technology changed your life?
- Do you 'own' it or does it 'own' you?
- What has the impact been on your community?

Housing: The Community Crash Pad program is an extension of the so-called Granny-Flat program of the 1990's where Portland was encouraging the creation of additional living units in the City. That program didn't show great results, in part because it was interpreted so narrowly as housing for elderly parents. Now, however, we have government pushing for higher density, communities resisting in-fill that changes the look of the community, the aging Baby Boomers who will want to stay in their homes, Portland State University struggling to find enough housing for students, and other social challenges. I wondered if, with a little more government support, if a CCP might solve some of these problems.

Many municipalities are struggling with these same challenges: growing populations, homelessness, affordable housing, and sprawl.

• How is your community dealing with these problems?
• Could something like a CCP work in your community?
• If not, what could?

Chapter 2: Culture Shock

Group exercise: Draw a diagram similar to the one below, with a simplistic house, yard and street. Then figure out how you could keep and use all the rainwater on the site so that you could eliminate all the pipes (water, sewage, stormwater) coming into and out of the property.

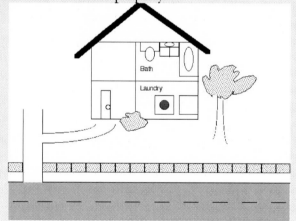

See if you can find out how much water you use each month. Hypothetically, do you get enough rain in your area that hits your roof to meet all your water needs?

Climate Change: Joe alludes to increasing storms on the east coast affecting air travel. This is intended as an allusion to one effect of climate change. For more information about the science of climate change, see reports by the Intergovernmental Panel on Climate Change or read *The Weathermakers*, my favorite book on the subject.

- What changes have you already seen?
- What fears do you have about the future?
- Why has it been so hard to get real action and what can be done about it?

Transportation Policy: Bus rapid transit has been in use in Curitiba, Brazil for many decades, a city of over 2 million. It's so efficient that more than half the trips taken by citizens there are by public transportation. And the fares pay the full cost of the system that is managed by the municipality but run by several different private companies. On a visit there in 2004, I didn't encounter a single traffic jam. Rush hour is a long line of people waiting to get on a bus, which during peak periods come every 56 seconds and can carry hundreds of passengers. There is a commitment to provide service at least every 15 minutes everywhere in the city; any less is inconvenient and reduces ridership. The city has given people a priority over cars, so everything is walk-able. Urban planning and transportation planning are done in concert so major transportation corridors flow down through the high-density areas, using existing streets, not expensive new highways.

- Why do you think it has taken the United States so long to invest in public transportation?
- What are the relative benefits and drawbacks of bus rapid transit and light rail?
- If you were to design a system for your community, where would you put the major and secondary transit corridors? How would this likely affect development?

Green streets and storm water: Green streets in Seattle, Washington, handled heavy rains without overloading the storm water system. Green streets usually involve eliminating curbs or providing curb cuts so that the rainwater is diverted to bioswales instead of the storm water system. They may also include pervious pavement and native plants. Well planned, these 'storm water gardens' can be aesthetically beautiful, adding habitat for birds, butterflies and other species. Some green streets put the walkways between the houses, away from the road. For more information about green streets, see Green Street Manual from the Charles River Watershed Association.

One of the main benefits of green streets is that they capture and treat rainwater.

- How much money do you think your community pays in sewer fees and other costs related to storm water?
- What would you rather do with that money?
- How could you incorporate the concepts of green streets into your neighborhood?

Chapter 3: Trash Talk

For an interesting depiction of the impact our consumption and waste have on the world, go to www.storyofstuff.com and watch the 20 min video.

Group exercise:
To prepare for this exercise, do this at home or work:
1. First estimate what you think will be your largest waste categories and how much by weight you generate in one week. Use or modify these categories: recycled paper, waste paper, recycled metals, recycled plastics, recycled glass, food waste,
2. Then separate your trash for one week and weigh each category. Bring your data to the meeting.

When you meet, share your data. How much is paper, food waste, recyclable cans/bottles/plastics? What ended up in the trash that could have been recycled? Which is the largest category? What surprised you?

It can be helpful to use a worksheet like the sample below.

Category	Estimate (weight or ranking)	Actual (weight or ranking)	Difference
Recycled			
Paper			
Metals			
Glass			
Plastics			
Food waste (composted)			
Not recycled			
Paper			
Metals			
Glass			
Plastic			
Food waste			
Other (specify)			

Alternative exercise: Do a waste sort of a representative sample of your trash (at home or work). Use gloves and separate the waste into plastic buckets that are labeled with their weight. You may have to discuss categories. Is ketchup food waste or liquid? When you're done, weigh the buckets, subtracting the weight of the buckets themselves. What percentage of your waste is being recycled? What could you do to recycle more and reduce your total waste (including recyclables)?

Waste: In this chapter, we take on the issue of waste. A number of companies have already achieved zero waste to landfill, meaning they have no dumpsters going to the dump. Typically, a vast majority of the material is reused, recycled or sold to another company for use in their process. A small percentage may be burned for power. Most organizations have saved money in the process.

- Why haven't more organizations eliminated the concept of waste so that they see everything as a resource?
- What are your largest waste streams?
- What could be done with it?
- What are the barriers to zero waste and what could be done?

Alternative Transportation: Tess bikes to some of her clients. Portland happens to be known as one of the more bike-able communities. A number of professionals bike at least part of the year. This is, of course, only one form of alternative transportation.

- What adjustments would you have to make to use some form of alternative transportation to get to work: walking, biking, taking the bus/train, etc.?
- How might this affect your health, your frame of mind, or the amount of time you have to yourself?
- Can you imagine getting rid of one household car (or company fleet vehicle) and using a car sharing service?
- How much money might you save if you did?

Group exercise: On a large piece of paper, make a rough map of your neighborhood (perhaps a five mile radius). Go through the following categories and ask people to share their favorite places: restaurants, parks, walks, clothing stores, markets, daycare facilities, baby sitters, vets, bike routes, etc. Mark these on the map. The purpose of this exercise is to build a map of community resources to encourage walking and biking.

Chapter 4: Local Economy

Urban Livestock: Emily raises ducks for eggs in her backyard which she sells using the local currency.
- What do you think about having small livestock in the city?
- What are the risks and benefits?

Local Currencies: Beaumont Bucks are an invention but local currencies are nothing new. A number of communities have them.
- If you have a local currency, how might this affect your shopping habits as well as the health of your community and local economy?
- What 5 services might you offer to your neighbors?
- Since the currencies work best if people don't hoard them, what services might you avail yourself of that you don't now?
- Do you think it would feel different to trade a local currency for services than dollars (or whatever your national currency is)?

Economics and Well-being: Emily rails about traditional economics, which don't take into account ecosystem services that are 'free' but essential. Herman Daly created the Genuine Progress Indicator where he subtracted from the GDP negative expenses such as the costs associated with prisons and environmental clean-up. (See the article in the Atlantic Monthly, "If the GDP is up, why is America Down.") Bhutan has a Gross Happiness Indicator. And in Mark Aneilski's book, *The Economics of Happiness,* includes a Genuine Wealth Assessment.

- Do you think the commonly reported economic measures (like GDP, job growth or the stock market performance) are accurate reflections of our well-being?
- If not, what could you use instead?
- What are the aberrations that traditional economics have caused that drive us away instead of toward sustainability?

Chapter 5: Breaking Bread

Neighborliness: Tess's neighborhood has built a strong sense of community and connection, in part by having monthly potlucks.

- What are the advantages that a community like hers has over typical American urban neighborhoods?
- How strong is your community?
- How might you benefit from a stronger community and what could you do to begin the process of building social capital?

Lending 'Libraries': Ralph manages the tool lending library, an informal mechanism for the neighbors to share tools.

- Why do so many people feel the need to own their own hand tools and lawnmowers when they are infrequently used?
- How could you envision something like this working?
- What problems might ensue and how could you deal with them productively?
- What else other than tools might this concept be applied to?

Rainwater Collection: Ralph and Ginny, as well as others in the neighborhood, capture rainwater for their household. While the RainWorm is an invention of my imagination, the other systems are real and a number of houses in Portland have been legally permitted to use rainwater for everything including potable drinking water. Most have large buried tanks and a UV treatment to kill any bacteria.

- How did we come to have central water facilities?
- As the infrastructure in all cities disintegrates and as populations grow, could rainwater catchment be at least part of the solution?
- What problems are generated by all the impervious surfaces when it rains in your community that might be averted if at least a portion of the rain were captured?

Distributed Energy: This chapter also alludes to distributed energy. In the past, energy generation has been in large, centralized power plants sited far from major population centers. Unfortunately, this leads to line-loss and the heat generated in the process is not put to good use. In Europe, combined heat and power plants are located close to homes and factories where the heat can be used. As we transition to more renewable energy sources, we're likely to have increasingly distributed and varied energy generation: solar cells on homes, wind turbines on ridges, and biomass plants burning our garbage. If you want to learn more about whether renewable energy can pencil out while allowing us to maintain our standard of living, read *Heat: How to Stop the Planet from Burning* by George Monbiot.

- What renewable energy sources might be important in the future in your region (e.g., solar, geothermal, wind, wave, or tidal)? Is enough being done to develop these sources?
- Do you think we can generate enough to maintain our lifestyle?
- If not, how could you radically improve energy conservation?

Chapter 6: Connected Communities

Housing: This chapter looks at home size as one indicator of materialism. The average number of square feet per person for housing has been rising steadily in the US since World War II. In many cases, homes that used to house a whole family may have only one or two people living there.

- What's been pushing the trend toward larger houses, fancier bathrooms, extra entertainment rooms and the like?

- Take one room and do a quick inventory of the original purchase price of the items in it. Now multiply that by the number of rooms in your house. How many months or years do you have to work to pay for all that stuff?

- Why do you have all of it? What percentage of it did you actively use in the last month or year?

- What would it feel like to give 1/3 of it away to others who would use it?

- We're often reminded that consumer spending is two-thirds of our economy. What would a healthy economy look like that wasn't addicted to our take-make-waste cycle, depleting our natural resources?

Aging Population: This chapter also alludes to the aging population of Baby Boomers in the US, although many developed nations face the same demographic shift. Boomer Roomers is a term I made up but there are groups of people who have lived this way in various communities. For an intriguing trend, learn about co-housing.

- What changes do you think the aging demographics will bring to our society?

- What do you think are the optimal living conditions for people as they age?

- What do you envision wanting for yourself as you age and what would need to happen to make that possible?

Chapter 7: Anti-Toxin

It's shocking the chemicals that are in perfectly legal products. If you're curious why I picked on vinyl shower curtains, download the executive summary of *Volatile Vinyl: The New Shower Curtain's Chemical Smell*. http://www.chej.org/showercurtainreport/

Body Burden: Most people are oblivious to the toxic chemicals in various products, everything from household cleaners and cosmetics as well as garden and home improvement products. At work, people are exposed to chemicals from whiteboard markers and printers, some of which are reportedly as bad to be around as smokers. When people do learn about this, many just shrug and go on.

- What has led to this apathy?
- What led us to develop positive associations with that new-car smell and 'mountain-fresh scent'?
- What products are you aware of that contain toxic chemicals?
- What alternatives have you tried and do they work?
- What would it take to raise body burden to the same level of awareness as second-hand smoke?
- What do you think government and businesses should be doing to address these problems?

For more information see *Exposed: The Toxic Chemistry of Everyday Products, and What's at Stake for American Power* by Mark

Shapiro and *Having Faith* or *Living Downstream* two books by Barbara Steingrabber.

Eating Local and In Season: Joe is frustrated because he can't buy bananas, which he is used to eating. There is a trend toward eating organic, local and in-season. Farmers Markets are one manifestation of this. Someone even coined a new term—locavore—to describe someone who eats locally. For more about this, read *Animal, Vegetable, Miracle* by Barbara Kingsolver.

- When you do grocery shopping or eat out, what factors into your buying decisions?
- What do you know about various certifications (organic, Food Alliance, Marine Stewardship Council, Free Trade, etc.) and which ones are credible and meaningful to you?
- Are you willing to pay more for these agricultural products? Why or why not?

Meditation and Spirituality: Meditation, yoga, qigong and tai chi are no longer just practices for the New Age set. Western medicine is beginning to value these practices and more data is amassing about their value. Some schools and workplaces are encouraging these practices because they enhance productivity. For a fascinating glimpse into the application of spiritual practice in a workplace setting, read *Presence* by MIT professor Peter Senge [and others].

- How well do you take care of yourself (exercise, nutrition, work-life balance, etc.) and how does this affect those around you?
- Do you have a practice that helps you manage stress, gain insights, and feel content?
- If so, what has your experience been? What has been difficult or fulfilling about it? What break-throughs have you experienced?
- What other practices are you curious about?
- How might our society be different if the majority of people regularly participated in such a practice?

Chapter 8—Harvest Barnstorm

Farming and Migrant Labor: Agri-tainment is already a phenomenon and to some degree, it involves harvesting produce (e.g., you-pick strawberries). But in developed nations, it is not common for the general public to get involved with planting, caring for or harvesting most of what we eat. Because of the reluctance of citizens to work full-time in the agriculture, many countries import labor, legally and illegally, to do this difficult work. The Harvest Barnstorm is one idea for reconnecting our largely urban population to the land.

- Do you and your kids know where most of your food comes from?
- What are the impacts of our urban population being disconnected with nature and rural communities?
- Could something like the Harvest Barnstorms work? Why or why not?
- How might it change your views if you adopted a farm (vegetables, fruits, and/or livestock) and worked there a few times a year?

Corporate Strategy: Ollie and Ann expose Joe to the evolution in their thinking about the future role of their business. It can be useful to think in three timeframes: near-term, how to clean up your existing operation; intermediate-term, what your organization's role could be to move us toward a sustainable society; and long-term, what your role might be in a fully-sustainable society.

- Pick an industry you think is currently the antithesis of sustainability (e.g., mining, oil drilling). How might they redeploy their core competence to support rather than detract from sustainability?
- How is the industry you work for (or major industries in your community) likely to be affected by trends associated with sustainability? What are threats and opportunities?
- What is you and/or your organization uniquely positioned to contribute to moving us toward a sustainable future?

Chapter 9—Investing in the Future

Investments: Socially responsible investing has been around for well over a decade. At first, it was a matter of applying 'negative screens' to weed out companies associated with tobacco, defense and the like. Then it involved 'positive screens' to select companies that shared your values. The problem was that there were no universally held values. Were homosexual rights a good thing or a bad thing? Different people held different views. Now some mutual fund companies such as Pax World are focusing on sustainable investing, where sustainability helps to link global trends to corporate strategy. Also the Carbon Disclosure Project is forcing companies to divulge their risks associated with climate change. So sustainability is making it's way into shareholder meetings and corporate boardrooms.

- Do your investments (personal or corporate) reflect your values?
- Do you assume you need to give up return to invest with your values?
- How is sustainability likely to affect the future of the industries you're most closely tied to (through your job or investments)?
- Do you think that Wall Street can ever be aligned with sustainability? Why or why not?

Chapter 10—Time and Money

Work-Life Balance: According to research, happiness and income are not correlated once you go beyond a very basic level of income. In our society, it seems we're hell-bent to work harder to get more stuff which means we have to work harder to pay it all off. We go into debt and pay for storage facilities to hold all the stuff we accumulate. But all this stuff hasn't made us happier than we were back in the 1950's, yet now most parents both have to work just to make ends meet. In contrast, some sociologists have estimated that many indigenous cultures have a 3-hour workday. That's the time it takes them to gather and prepare food and do other chores. To learn more, read *The High Price of Materialism* by Tim Kasser; *The*

Overworked American: The Unexpected Decline of Leisure, The Overspent American: Why We Want What We Don't Need, and Born to Buy: The Commercialized Child and the New Consumer Culture by Juliet Schor; and *Affluenza* (video).

- What is driving our desire to accumulate material possessions?
- What would you be willing to give up to have more time for your family and community?
- Calculate all the money you spend in a year on things that don't add *significantly* to your sense of well-being. Add up the market value of the possessions (clothing, electronics, dishes, etc.) that you rarely use. How long did you have to work (after taxes) to pay for all this? What would it feel like to give it away?
- What contributes to a sense of well-being and contentment?

Population: Tess reveals that she would rather adopt but Joe can't believe he won't have his 'own' grandchildren. Population control is a sensitive, taboo subject in our society. No one wants to resort to draconian measures to prevent or terminate pregnancies, yet the pressure our population growth has put on nature is undeniable. Gretchen Daily, in her book, The Stork and the Plow, makes the case that in many underdeveloped countries, one of the most effective means of reducing population growth is to focus on women's rights, access to healthcare and family planning, and education. Some developed nations are at the same time struggling with a stagnant birthrates and/or conflicts associated with immigration.

- Why is it so hard for us to discuss population issues?
- What is contributing to population growth in your region and what effects have you witnessed?
- What might encourage people to delay pregnancy, to adopt, or to choose a childless lifestyle without infringing on individual rights?

Healthcare: In this chapter, the conflict between Tess and Joe come to a head. The healthcare system and Joe's employer let them all down. Carol gave up and took her own life; Joe couldn't take a leave of absence without losing his coverage; and all this time, Tess thought her father shouldn't have left her mother alone that day.

In what ways do you see our healthcare system has let us down?

What would you think should be done?

What do you think about how society often deals with end-of-life issues?

Chapter 11—Exploring the Commons

Tragedy of the commons: The commons are those things that are not privately owned but benefit many. However, without strong social norms regarding managing the commons, we tend to over-exploit them. Public lands may become overgrazed, fisheries over-harvested. Individuals tend to act in ways meant to maximize their own benefits but the combined effect is to deplete the resource for all. Climate change is yet another example, where developed nations have exploited fossil fuels to raise the standard of living and developing nations consider it unfair now to limit their ability to develop in the same way.

- What examples of the tragedy of the commons have you witnessed?

- What is the common response by government, business and the public to these types of situations?

- What agreements or group norms would be necessary to manage the commons fairly and sustainably?

- Regarding climate change, one proposal called Contraction and Convergence involves setting a scientifically-based global limit on greenhouse gases and then allocating a share to each person on the planet. Over time, people in poor countries might increase their per capita greenhouse gases and those in rich nations could, for a time, buy shares from others if they want to exceed their limit. Can you see this working?

Homelessness: The causes of homelessness are complex but our inability to provide shelter to all our citizens is shameful. When I visited Curitiba, Brazil, I didn't see a single homeless person or smell a urine-soaked alleyway. This is in part because they have a three-digit phone number similar to 911 that dispatches a van and social worker to offer assistance to anyone in need. The municipality maintains relationships with a host of charitable organizations that provide targeted services: emergency food, alcohol/drug treatment, counseling for run-away youth, etc. In this country, Seattle and other communities are experimenting with providing housing first and working to resolve other problems later. I got the example of the perverse incentive (needing to get blitzed so as not to be put out on the street in the middle of the night) from a documentary on these programs.

- How much of an issue is homelessness in your community?
- What do you know about the demographics of the homeless? For example, what percentage are families on hard times versus people with mental illness or chronic drug and alcohol problems?
- How would you explain to someone of another country why we allow this to continue in the US, the richest nation on earth?
- What do you think should be done?

Chapter 12—Natural High

Group exercise: Take out a map of your state or province. Ask each person to mark on the map (use Post-It's if you don't want to write on the map) where their favorite place is and explain why. Reflect on how many of these places are natural as opposed to the built-environment. Typically this exercise leads to other people wanting to visit your favorite place so it can help to come prepared to explain how to get there. (For example, people who love to fish sometimes share GPS readings.)

Biophilia: Joe, on his hike up Mount Hood, connects deeply with nature. A number of research studies suggest that humans need this connection for their own well-being. Biophilia is a new term to describe this human need. However, in the past few years, the majority of people now live in urban environments, increasingly disconnected from nature.

- When did you feel most connected to nature? When was that and what did you experience?
- How does our society's lack of connection to nature manifest itself?
- What are the long-term implications if this continues?
- What can be done to provide the opportunity for everyone to enjoy and appreciate nature?

Chapter 13—Sustainable Business

Finding your niche: Tess and her father first generate a business idea that Tess is not well positioned to fulfill. It takes them some time to uncover a role that is better suited to who she is and what they, together, have to offer. I have conducted countless informational interviews with people wanting to get into the sustainability field. In many cases, these people assume they necessarily have to go back to school or make a huge shift in their lives. Instead, I try to uncover their unique talents and interests and then help them find a place where they can uniquely contribute to the sustainability movement. The field is so broad and the needs are so great, there is I believe a place for everyone at the table.

- What do you love to do?
- What social, economic and/or environmental issues concern you the most?
- What skills and abilities do you possess?
- What work environments best suit your needs?
- Where do these intersect with the sustainability field? What are you uniquely prepared to contribute to society?

Research and development: We are witnessing a sea-change in our society. We know from history that this has often up-ended winners and losers. Entirely new industries emerge and mature ones wane. New, disruptive technologies have far-reaching effects. It helps, during times of turbulent change, to have an understanding of the changes afoot, both to protect your own organization and the future of your career. Often, synergies develop between a couple industries. Think about the powerful changes brought by the information technology revolution of the last century, driven by improvements in semi-conductors, software, and telephony. I believe that clean-tech may play a similar role in the future, driven by advancements in energy production, water conservation, transportation systems and nanotechnology in response to concerns about climate change, pollution, and natural resources depletion. See *The Clean-Tech Revolution* by Ron Pernick and Clint Wilder for more information.

- What are the industries that you think will be main players in the next 20 years? Why?
- How could these be combined to solve world problems?
- What are possible unintended side-effects?
- Where are there intriguing opportunities that these changes create?

Chapter 14—Considering Commitment

Significant others: Joe encourages Tess to consider the value of a long-term partner. With roughly half of marriages ending in divorce, it may seem quaint. A marriage based on love is a fairly recent development, one that is still resisted in places like India. In the Western world, we hold quite high expectations for our marriage partner.

- What has your experience been with long-term relationships? In what ways have they contributed to (or detracted from) your well-being?
- Our society is much more accepting now of divorce than it used to be several decades ago. Overall, do you think this has improved or detracted from the well-being of our society? What have we gained and lost?
- Our society is filled with stories that perpetuate the idea that there is a perfect man or woman out there for you. What has led to the longevity of this cultural story? In what ways has it manifested in your life? Do you believe it or not?

Your calling: The dragonfly's question prompts us all to find a purpose in life. You are more than your job, your roles, or your heritage. The problems of our time challenge us all to take action. We live in a unique moment in time. We know the problems we are creating. We, to a large degree, know what needs to be done. Many of the technologies are already available or soon to be economically viable. The only question is whether we have the vision, the moral compass, and the political will to change. There is no one else to do this work. And if we don't, think how hollow our excuses will sound to our children. The thesis of this book is that many of these changes are not sacrifices but rather a path to a better, more fulfilling life.

- What ideas from this book might improve the livability of your community and the well-being of your family?
- What are you willing to do to reduce your negative impacts on the environment and social justice?
- How can you get others excited about doing their part?
- What are you doing here?

Action Plan

Use this space in the book to make a plan for change.

Things I want to learn more about:

_____

_____

_____

_____

Things I will change at home:

_____

_____

_____

_____

Things I will change at work:

_____

_____

_____

_____

What are you doing here? What are you uniquely positioned to contribute to a better, more sustainable world?

_____

_____

_____

_____

About the Author

Darcy Hitchcock is a sustainability consultant and author of the award-winning book, *The Business Guide to Sustainability*, as well as five other business books. She is co-founder of AXIS Performance Advisors and the International Society of Sustainability Professionals. She also teaches at the prestigious Bainbridge Graduate Institute MBA in Sustainable Business and has co-hosted the Sustainable Today TV show.

Darcy wrote this novella because she believes in the transformative power of stories. Most people assume that to live a more sustainable life would require unacceptable sacrifice. But the sacrifices we're making in our existing, hectic culture have gone unexamined. By showing the two worlds through her two main character's points of view, she uncovers the contrast. With this book, Darcy wanted to show citizens and employees how sustainability could help us move toward a better, more satisfying and productive life. She lives in the Pacific Northwest with her husband and two dogs. If you want to share your thoughts about this discussion course and novella, you can reach her at darcy@axisperformance.com.